Navigating the Bible

Reading Without Getting Lost

Dr. Will Thomas

Dedicated to the saints of Saybrook and LeRoy Christian Churches who pointed me to Jesus, taught me to know and love God's Word, and encouraged me in my journey of faith and ministry.

Table of Contents

The Books of the Bible and Their Abbreviations.........................i

Epigraph iii

Preface v

   Going Deeper ix

   Going Deeper—Preface x

Chapter 1: Opening the Bible..1

   How to Buy a Bible 2

   Chapter and Verse 5

   Considering a Digital Bible 6

   Those Extra Items 6

   A Bible Reader's Starting Point...................................7

   Beginning at the Beginning..8

   Lesson Learned from Reading My Bible............................11

   Going Deeper—Chapter 1 12

Chapter 2: A Tale of Two Testaments 13

   A New Covenant Promised..15

   Do Christians Need the Old Testament? 17

   The First Christians and the Old Testament Issue 20

   Keeping Jews and Non-Jews in the Same Church 21

   The Best Treasure 22

   Going Deeper—Chapter 2 23

Chapter 3: The Story of God 24

Chapter One: Creation 26

Chapter Two: Conflict..28

Chapter Three: Covenant 29

Chapter Four: Christ 31

Chapter Five: The Co-Mission 33

Chapter Six: The Coronation...............................35

Going Deeper—Chapter 3 37

Chapter 4: Lessons from the Library 39

The Most Important Unknown Verse.....................40

Those Extra Books...41

The Combination that Unlocks the Old Testament Library ...43

What Makes Poetry Poetry 44

Fore-telling and Forth-telling................................47

Jesus Fulfills the Old Testament 48

Going Deeper—Chapter 4 50

Chapter 5: The Big Story...51

The Big Story—The Story of Israel.......................51

Where the Story of Israel Begins 52

The Preface to the Story of Israel 53

Genesis 12-50: The Introduction to the Story of Israel 55

The Story of Israel in Eight Chapters....................56

Going Deeper—Chapter 5 63

Chapter 6: The Jesus Story...64

The New Testament Library..66

The Fourfold Gospel 67

Different Gospels for Different Folks...................................68

Four Gospels: One Story...69

His Prophetic Birth..70

His Exemplary Life 71

His Amazing Miracles..72

His Challenging Teachings 72

His Atoning Death 73

His Victorious Resurrection..74

His Glorious Ascension and Heavenly Ministry......................75

His Promised Return 76

Going Deeper—Chapter 6 78

Chapter 7: The Story of the First Christians 79

Luke's Story: Volume Two 80

They Were First Called Christians..82

From Jerusalem to the World 83

The First Christian's Top Ten 84

The Legacy of the First Christians.......................................90

Going Deeper—Chapter 7 92

Chapter 8: Letters to the Frontlines 93

Churches as Battle Stations 94

Why We Need the Letters 94

Letters Old and New 95

The Authors of the Letters to the Frontline.......................96

Sorting the Letters to the Frontlines.......................97

Why the Letters Were Written.......................97

The Warriors to Whom the Letters Were   Written 99

The Message to the Frontlines 100

Going Deeper—Chapter 8 102

Chapter 9: The Grand Finale.......................104

Beginning at the Beginning.......................105

A Special Type of Book.......................109

Four Views of This One Book 111

What We Know and Don't Know 112

How the Story Ends.......................114

A Parting Word 116

Going Deeper—Chapter 9 118

Chapter 10: Confessions of a Bible Reader.......................119

I Don't Read the Bible Because.......................120

I Read the Bible Because.......................122

Going Deeper—Chapter 10 125

Appendix 1: How to Study the Bible 126

　Going Deeper—Appendix 1 131

Appendix 2: How to Teach the Bible....................................132

　How Adults Learn 132

　How Teachers Teach 134

　No Easy Road 136

　Going Deeper—Appendix 2 137

Appendix 3: Sharing Our Faith....................................138

　Telling Our Story of Hope 138

　Pray for Opportunities....................................139

　Building Bridges of Hope 139

　Moving Across the Bridge....................................139

　Sharing the Good News of Jesus with Clarity....................................141

　The Next Steps in the Journey....................................143

　Going Deeper—Appendix 3 144

Endnotes....................................145

About the Author....................................146

The Books of the Bible and Their Abbreviations

The Old Testament Library

Books of Law

Genesis	Gn
Exodus	Ex
Leviticus	Lv
Numbers	Nm
Deuteronomy	Dt

Books of History

Joshua	Jo
Judges	Jgs
Ruth	Ru
1 Samuel	1 Sm
2 Samuel	2 Sm
1 Kings	1 Kgs
2 Kings	2 Kgs
1 Chronicles	1 Chr
2 Chronicles	2 Chr
Ezra	Ezr
Nehemiah	Neh
Esther	Est

Books of Poetry

Job	Jb
Psalms	Pss
Proverbs	Prv
Song of Solomon	Sg
Ecclesiastes	Eccl

The Major Prophets

Isaiah	Is
Jeremiah	Jer
Lamentations	Lam
Ezekiel	Ez
Daniel	Dn

The Minor Prophets

Hosea	Hos
Joel	Jl
Amos	Am
Obadiah	Ob
Jonah	Jon
Micah	Mi
Nahum	Na
Habakkuk	Hb
Zephaniah	Sep
Haggai	Hg
Zechariah	Zec
Malachi	Mal

The New Testament Library

Gospels

Matthew	Mt
Mark	Mk
Luke	Lk
John	Jn

History

Acts of the Apostles	Acts

Epistles

Romans	Rm
1 Corinthians	1 Cor
2 Corinthians	2 Cor
Galatians	Gal
Ephesians	Eph
Philippians	Phil
Colossians	Col
1 Thessalonians	1 Thes
2 Thessalonians	2 Thes
1 Timothy	1 Tm
2 Timothy	2 Tm
Titus	Ti
Philemon	Phlm
Hebrews	Heb
James	Jas
1 Peter	1 Pt
2 Peter	2 Pt
1 John	1 Jn
2 John	2 Jn
3 John	3 Jn
Jude	Jude

Prophecy

Revelation	Rv

Epigraph

God's Word is better than a diamond,
better than a diamond set between emeralds.
You'll like it better than strawberries in spring,
better than red, ripe strawberries.
Psalm 19:10 (The Message).

And beginning with Moses and all the Prophets, he [Jesus]
explained to them what was said in all the Scriptures concerning
himself.
Luke 24:27 (NIV).

You have been taught the Holy Scriptures from childhood, and they
have given you the wisdom to receive the salvation that comes by
trusting in Christ Jesus. All Scripture is inspired by God and is
useful to teach us what is true and to make us realize what is wrong
in our lives. It corrects us when we are wrong and teaches us to do
what is right. God uses it to prepare and equip his people to do
every good work.
2 Timothy 3:15-17 (NLT).

Preface

The Bible is an amazing book by any standard. It's a big book, the biggest that many of us will ever think of reading. This one volume contains sixty-six different books, penned by at least forty authors over a span of nearly 1500 years. Despite its intimating size, the Bible remains the best-selling book in the world. It is estimated that 100 million copies are printed each year, leaving approximately six billion in print. Americans buy nearly 20 million Bibles each year. Run the numbers, that's 6.4 Bibles sold every 10 seconds!

But the Bible has a problem—there are far more Bible owners than Bible readers! Lots are purchased, far fewer are read, and far fewer than that are understood! For too many, the Bible is a confusing book. It is confusing to both strangers and veterans.

When I say stranger, I am referring to someone who has never been exposed to the Bible. He may never have attended Sunday School as a child or dropped out when overwhelmed by the angst of the teenage years. He might have grown up in a secular home where church and religion never played any role in daily life. The Bible is a total mystery. Most strangers aren't antagonistic toward the Bible. They don't know enough about it to care.

But sometimes, the situation changes. This stranger to the Bible runs into a believer they grow to respect. They listen to them talk about the Bible and wonder what it's all about. Somebody may give them a Bible or they buy one for themselves out of curiosity. Maybe they simply thumb through the Gideon Bible they find in a hotel room. They read a verse or two. They put the book down, wondering what all the fuss is about. They don't get it.

For whatever reason, strangers sometimes become seekers. They decide maybe they are missing something. Perhaps, it's triggered by a personal crisis. It could be anything—sickness, sorrow, maybe even guilt. They sense a hunger for something "spiritual" in their lives. They have been told they can find what they are looking for in the Bible. They pick up the Bible seriously, wanting to understand what's in it. They try to read it. They may persist for a bit, but eventually, most give up. They just can't make sense of it. *Navigating the Bible: Reading Without Getting Lost* is for them.

On a totally different level, many veteran churchgoers could find benefits in the following pages. Most veteran churchgoers are not strangers to the Bible. They would probably be offended if you said they were. They may own several Bibles. They listen to it read at church. They may even discuss it with others in classes or small groups. But, if the truth were told, most of them seldom read the Bible themselves. When they do, most often, it is only a verse or two that accompanies a devotional book. The devotional leads them from a verse here to a verse there and then offers a spiritual pep talk. Other than that, their Bibles remain closed on the nightstand or the table by their easy chair.

Many of these folk I know are sincere believers. They hold dear the beliefs they hear at church. They believe in the Bible. They simply don't *read it.* They intend to. They make plans for every New Year. They may even start. But all too quickly, the good intentions give way to reality. They don't read the Bible because they don't really understand it. They conclude that the Bible is way too complicated for normal people. It's best left to the clergy.

Why do so many people, both strangers and discouraged believers, give up on reading the Bible? Sometimes it is because of *how* they read it. They open the Bible randomly, read a verse or two, open to another spot, read a few more verses, and put the book down. And they wonder why it doesn't make sense! Even some popular Bible reading plans skip hither and yon, front to back, and leave readers discouraged by their confusion. Just reading the Bible regularly *in context* would help, but even that is sometimes not enough.

Maybe a big reason many people give up on reading their Bibles or don't understand it when they do—they get lost. They wander around without any sense of where they are or where they are going. They don't understand the Bible because they need a map. I don't mean the colorful pages printed at the back of some Bibles that identify the oceans, mountains, countries, and cities. I am talking about a roadmap for the Bible itself.

Someone suggested to me not long ago that they wished they had a GPS for their Bible. As you know, a GPS is that app on your phone or the high-tech feature in your car that keeps you on course. The GPS tracks your location at any given point and lays out the route ahead. The GPS coaches a driver to turn at the right point or completely turn around when he's veered off course. Without the GPS, a person can unknowingly make a wrong turn and end up heading in the opposite direction. We've all been there! *Navigating the Bible: Reading Without Getting Lost* offers a GPS for the Bible.

Too often, even veteran readers travel through the Bible learning tons of facts. They are like a tourist driving to and fro, looking at the sites but never paying any attention to the route itself. As a result, they have no idea about where they have been or where they are going. A driver who finally realizes he is aimlessly wandering around would eventually give up and try to head for home. That's what happens to many Bible readers. They wander around for a while and when they realize they are getting nowhere, they give up. The only difference between strangers and discouraged veterans—the strangers give up sooner. The veterans keep going out of a sense of obligation or even guilt!

This lack of a sense of how the Bible works, the storyline, and the connectivity between the events also leads to misunderstandings. The most common distortion is the belief in a "level Bible." Without understanding the differences between the two testaments, a reader can easily fail to keep the main thing the main thing. For example, the significance of the cross and resurrection can get lost in a mountain of stories about people, places, and events. The Good News of Jesus shrinks to the same level as the story of David and Goliath. Leviticus's purity laws become as important as the Sermon on Mount. Nothing could be more devastating for a firm grasp of the Gospel.

Discouraged Bible readers become non-Bible-readers. A church of non-Bible readers leads to one without a foundation or a direction. No church lasts long without direction and purpose. If that direction doesn't come from Scripture, it will come from somewhere else— tradition, culture, politics, or whichever direction the latest winds are blowing. Does that sound like a church, you know?

In the pages that follow, you will learn to *navigate the Bible without getting lost.* I want you to begin, even if you are a veteran Bible reader, as if you have picked up a Bible for the very first time. Look at it with fresh eyes! We will begin by looking at the cover and the table of contents. We will move to a discussion of why the Bible is divided into Old and New Testaments and what that means. We will look at the Bible as a whole and then the library of books that form it and how they are laid out. Eventually, we will move to the *Story of Jesus* and why that is the most important message of all. We will conclude by trying to wrap our heads around the grand finale to which the Bible points.

That's our roadmap! I hope you enjoy the journey.

***

Going Deeper

After each chapter in *Navigating the Bible*, you will find a series of assignments or questions. These are designed to deepen your understanding of "how the Bible works" and its application to your life. Reading each chapter of *Navigating the Bible* can be helpful, but thinking about it and working through its implications can take your experience to a whole new level. The assignments will prepare you for the next chapter and beyond in each case.

Keeping a notebook or journal in which to record your answers will prove valuable. As you write your thoughts and reread them in the future, your personal experience with the Bible will grow deeper and have a more lasting impact on your faith. Of course, these same questions can be used in a small group or class setting to stimulate discussion and shared learning.

Most *Going Deeper* sections contain one or more questions designed to kickstart small group discussion or serve as a jumping-off point for personal reflection. These questions are intended to "prime the pump" for thinking about a main idea in the material. Sometimes a scripture will be suggested to be read and reflected upon. Other times, a specific activity or assignment will be outlined that will either apply the material you have read or prepare you for what will come next.

The questions or assignments all seek to reinforce the "holy trinity" of biblical learning—information, inspiration, and transformation.

***

Going Deeper—Preface

1. What has been your experience with reading the Bible? How would you describe yourself? A beginner? A veteran? An outsider? Something else? When did your interest in the Bible first begin?

2. If you were to graph or draw a timeline depicting your personal efforts to read and understand the Bible over the years, when were the high points and the low points? Any explanation?

3. In the following pages, *Navigating the Bible* will explore how the Bible "works" and overview its contents. What do you hope to gain from this?

4. Before you turn to the next chapter, open the Bible you read the most. Your Bible will likely have a preface or introduction explaining items that the publisher thinks are important for you to know about this particular version of the Bible. Read the preface. What did you learn that you didn't know before? What do the publishers think makes this Bible different from others? Why do they think another Bible version is needed? What did you find most helpful in the preface? Did you find anything that confused you?

5. Think about how much of the Bible you would like to read in the next three months. Where would you like to start? How often would you intend to read the Bible? How much would you need to read each day or week to reach your goal? Develop a plan for when and where you will begin this journey.

Chapter 1: Opening the Bible

I remember receiving my first Bible. I was eight or ten years old. I don't remember exactly. Even though I don't remember the date, I remember the occasion as if it were yesterday. My parents took me on a shopping trip to the county seat town about thirty miles away. Eventually, we found our way to a stationary store just off the courthouse square. I am sure it's long gone. But I am convinced I could still find the spot where it once stood. That's how vivid the memory remains.

The small store sold stationery, of course, paper products, greeting cards, and an assortment of other items, including a few books and Bibles. My mother steered me toward the Bible section. We looked over a few and finally settled on a medium-sized King James Version. It had a flexible black cardboard cover that was pebbled to resemble leather. I have no idea how much it cost. But at the time, and still, to this day, it is one of my most priceless possessions.

I held it all the way home that day. I opened it, thumbed through its pages, read a verse here and there and reverently carried it to my bedroom. I loved that Bible. It changed my life and pointed me in directions I would never have known otherwise.

Since then, I have owned scores of Bibles in all kinds of versions. I have had expensive ones with fancy leather covers and cheap paperback copies. I later moved on from that first KJV Bible to a Revised Standard Version, then to an American Standard Version, and a bit later, the Good News Bible (TEV). Eventually, I settled into the NIV, the NASB, and the ESV as my Bibles of choice.

I have owned most of the different translations that have popped up from time to time. Early on, I realized that owning a Bible was not enough. I needed to read it. I read small sections at first and later larger and larger portions. Eventually, I would read it through. Now decades after receiving that first Bible, I have read the book from cover to cover scores of times.

I have learned a few things about the Bible through the years. I am convinced more than ever that owning a Bible is a great thing. Many of us have more than one. Some in other parts of the world look forward to owning their first Bible. But just owning a Bible is only the beginning. We need to read it. More than reading it, we need to understand it. If we understand the Bible, we need to acknowledge and submit to the One it tells us about and order our lives accordingly. That must always be the goal behind owning and reading our Bibles.

Let's begin at the beginning. That's always a good place to start. In this chapter, I want to cover a few often-overlooked basics. From there, we will move on to examining how the Bible is laid out. After that, we will look at the "big picture" that unites the entire Bible into one overarching story. Our goal will be to understand the Bible in its own context. That is our task; let's get started.

How to Buy a Bible

It has been years since I came home with that brand-new Bible under my arm. Since then, I have learned a few things about buying a Bible for myself. A fancy cover and delicate pages might look good, but it generally doesn't work well. A good sturdy cover is important. It doesn't have to be leather, though leather certainly wears well. The Bible's binding, whether glued or stitched, needs to be durable. Most Bibles endure some abuse. They are dropped, tossed, and stepped on. More than a few Bibles have been known to fall victim to the family dog or a spilled cup of coffee.

Fancy paper especially doesn't work well. If I intend to really use my Bible, I will want to be able to write in it, take notes during the sermon at church, or mark passages that I will come back to again and again. Thin paper bleeds through or tears too easily if I write quickly. The stronger the paper, the better the Bible!

Picking out a translation is another conundrum. I recommend the "read" one. READ, not red! Most modern translations are fairly accurate and understandable. Publishers keep coming up with new translations. It's hard to keep up. I have found that keeping up doesn't matter. I am satisfied to find a good translation and stay with it. However, I do find it helpful to try different translations from time to time. New wording and phrasing keep me from simply relying on the "tape" that runs in my head from a previous reading. I often switch translations when I begin a new trip reading through the whole Bible again.

New translations are needed for two reasons: 1) our language changes, and 2) over time, scholars have gained more and more understanding of ancient languages and customs. Bridging that ancient divide is a delicate blend of both science and art. Producing a translation that is both accurate and understandable presents a formidable task. Some translations would seem better at the accuracy part and others at the understandable side. A few claim to follow a "word for word" philosophy of translation, others what they call "dynamic equivalency." I have concluded that the difference is often overblown. Translation from any language into another never follows a strict word-for-word process. It's impossible. Each language has its own principles of grammar and syntax (word forms and order). But a translator's creativity must have limits. Where to draw that line is an issue that will likely not be settled any time soon.

Consider the over four-hundred-year-old King James Version. It was reasonably good in its day and has remained a classic ever since. Its influence on English culture and language can't be overstated. For that reason, Bible readers continue to value the KJV. But much has changed since 1611. The archaic and obscure words present unnecessary hurdles for most readers.

Who knows that "neesings" refers to a sneeze (Job 41:18). More than a few people have been confused because they didn't know that "suffer the little children" didn't mean to inflict pain. Four-hundred years ago, "suffer" meant allow (Mark 10:14). Of course, Paul didn't say that those alive at Christ's return would "prevent" those who had already died. "Prevent" meant "precede" back then (1 Thess 4:15). Or who knows what "fetch a compass" means (Acts 28:13)? It once referred to turning a sailing ship in the opposite direction. On and on, the examples could go. Choosing the KJV for the beauty of its language remains an option, but be prepared for some extra work.

The best translation is the one that you will read and look forward to reading again and again. I am personally more concerned about "how" you read the Bible than which translation you read. The Bible, just as anything important, should be read in context. Jumping from front to back, verse to verse, and splicing unrelated sentences together will likely be confusing at best and probably misleading. Beware of any Bible reading plan that encourages you to ignore the context and teaches you to copy and paste verses from here and there to understand what you find.

Chapter and Verse

One obvious difference between your Bible and most other books you will read is the presence of verse divisions. Human scholars created the verse and chapter divisions found in most Bibles. They are not a part of the original. But they are helpful. Imagine trying to locate a specific passage without a chapter and verse identifier or discussing a passage in a small group or class. An occasional publisher will offer Bibles with line numbers as opposed to verse numbers or no verse divisions at all. That makes the Bible look more like an ordinary book. That's not bad in itself. But I have found the lack of verse numbers more trouble than it's worth.

Most historians think the modern chapter divisions of the Bible were introduced in AD 1227 by Stephen Langton, Archbishop of Canterbury. Verse divisions came along a bit later. First, a Jewish rabbi by the name of Nathan divided the Hebrew Bible into verses around AD 1448. Robert Destine introduced the verse divisions to the New Testament in AD 1555. The popular Geneva Bible (1557-1560), the English version produced by British refugees who had fled to Switzerland during the persecution under Queen Mary I, became the first to use the chapter and verse divisions found in most modern versions. Almost every translation, regardless of publisher, continues to follow those same conventions.

The chapter and verse conventions provide a tremendous aid to Bible readers, but they are not infallible. Occasionally, you will find a division that interrupts the writer's train of thought. If you do, ignore the verse or chapter separation. Read on, following the flow and context as much as possible.

Considering a Digital Bible

In this day and age, more and more of us read the Bible on electronic devices. A few of us "dinosaurs" may argue for the superiority of an ink and paper Bible. It's probably a losing cause. I personally practice a hybrid approach. On my phone and other devices, I have a variety of translations, commentaries, and other study helps. But I still do my daily reading on a print Bible where I can mark, underline, and make notes for further reference. I know I could probably accomplish the same tasks on my digital Bible. This is probably a case of "old dogs and new tricks." The digital options will probably be second nature for future generations of Bible readers. Again, the main goal is to actually read the Bible. The format and the translation are not nearly as important.

Countless options are available for electronic Bibles. Readers can find almost any translation for their device, regardless of the brand or format of the phone, tablet, or computer. Many are free of charge. Also, the internet abounds with Bibles, Bible study helps, and commentaries. "Buyer beware" applies here as with everything else on the web. Bible readers need to continually distinguish between the contents of the Bible itself and human comments about it. This brings us to those "extras" we often find in our Bibles.

Those Extra Items

Many Bibles come with many helps included. These added features could be anything from maps, indexes, and simple dictionaries, all the way to complex commentaries. In every case, these are human additions, not part of the Bible. Most can be very helpful. Maps provide a context for the events described in the text of Scripture. Word indexes, or concordances, help locate a passage, find parallel passages, or enable you to follow a chain of usage throughout the Bible. Bible dictionaries usually refer to a discussion of topics rather than the simple definition of a word. Commentaries, of course, are the thoughts of human scholars and teachers. These can be quite helpful. But they are the product of human study and should not be considered the actual word of God or the last word, for that matter. The best commentaries acknowledge competing viewpoints and offer the reasoning behind their explanations.

These add-ons may be printed at the back of a Bible or on the same page with the Scripture text itself. Whether as a footnote, a chain reference printed between columns of the text, or other formats, these items should always be used with caution and an appropriate level of skepticism. Just because something appears on the same page as Scripture doesn't make it Scripture!

A Bible Reader's Starting Point

Where to begin when first reading the Bible has created a great deal of confusion. Often, new believers or curious seekers pick up a Bible and start reading. Assuming the Bible is a book like any other book, the typical new reader starts on page one. All is well for a while until the "newbie" hits the middle of Exodus or, at best, the first few pages of Leviticus. Often, the good intentions go out the window and the reader gives up on the Bible altogether. More than a few new Bibles have become dust catchers or paperweights after a few frustrating weeks. There has to be a better way.

I don't recommend starting at the front of the book, in Genesis. Instead, I suggest a new reader begin with one of the Gospels. Which one? Any of the four will do. But the best beginning point may depend on the person. I suggest that a person ask, "How do I see myself? Am I a doer, a thinker, a feeler, or a saver?" Or have a family member or good friend help tackle the question. These categories are loosely based on the "type and temperament" categories of the well-known Myers-Briggs Type Indicator and similar personality inventories. Without advocating any or all of the philosophy upon which the MBTI is based, I do think it provides some helpful categories for viewing observable differences in human personality.

Of course, thinkers do and doers think, as do feelers and savers. But in reality, some of us like to ponder things before we act. Others prefer to ponder as they do. Some are drawn to the human-interest element before anything else. They are easily moved by people and their problems. Still, others prefer to take things slow and make changes gradually. For doers, Mark provides a good starting point. Thinkers might be better served by starting with John, feelers with Luke, and savers with Matthew. This could be followed by one's second preference. The beginner can then move on to Acts and then the Letters. Eventually, the reader can turn to the Old Testament and the history that paved the path to Jesus. Without the Gospel, reading the Old Testament can be like looking through a veil (2 Cor 3:14-16). Only Christ can make the Old Testament make sense. However, where a person begins is not nearly as important as the fact that they begin AND continue reading the Bible.

Beginning at the Beginning

The Bible remains a popular book. Believers and seekers purchase millions of copies every year. Many resolve to read the Bible at the launch of each New Year. For most of these best-laid plans fizzle to a halt after a few weeks. Buying a Bible is simple. Most anyone can read it. Reading it regularly is another matter. Understanding the Bible remains a mystery for far too many. That's a problem that needs to be solved. But where to start?

An old story about Vince Lombardi, the legendary coach of the Green Bay Packers, provides a valuable illustration. After a particularly poor game, Lombardi supposedly gathered the team at the next practice to review how their play had gone. He grabbed a football, stood before the team and said, "Gentlemen, you know how you did Sunday. It wasn't a pretty picture. We need to work on our fundamentals. Let's start at the beginning. This is a football!"

Imagine you picked up a Bible for the first time. This is a Bible! What's the first thing you see? It is probably the words HOLY BIBLE. Bible simply means a book. Don't take that for granted. The ancients read from scrolls of leather. About the time of Jesus and a bit later, someone discovered a way to make paper. It would prove much lighter and easier to work with. The Chinese apparently had used something similar to paper for centuries. Eventually, Egyptians found a way to pound reeds into papyrus, an early form of paper. Around the same time, someone imagined that cutting the scrolls into manageable pages and binding them together on one side might improve matters. Indeed, it did. Eventually, we have the book. Later books moved from handwritten material to block printing.

In the 1400s, Guttenberg invented the moveable type. Modern printing and modern books were born. Soon books could be inexpensively copied and made accessible to the common man. Men and women could have their own Bibles. It is hard to imagine how big a revolution that was. Guttenberg's breakthrough pales in comparison to the revolution that has taken place around us in our lifetimes. Computers and the digital age have totally changed the way books are printed, copied, and distributed. Today, a device you can hold in your hand can contain the Bible in countless translations, plus all the study helps you could ever want. Our ancestors never imagined how owning and reading the Bible could be so easy.

The Bible is a book. But it is a special book. That's the meaning of the descriptive word "Holy." The word "Holy" carries the idea of being unique, devoted, and consecrated. In the case of the Bible, it emphasizes the idea that this book is something important and out of the ordinary. It is a book from and about God.

In our context, we understand what that means. The Living God inspired this book. It carries his message. In the context of other religions, many other books might be considered holy, and they are to those devoted to those religions. This is an important principle—context determines meaning. The same word can have a different meaning in a different context. In our context, the Holy Bible refers to this unique book that carries the message of the Living God. That book can transform our lives for eternity. It can do that because the Holy Bible points us to the Son of the Living God, revealed in the flesh and in history once and for all.

Before you open the Bible you hold in your hands, let's try something. Open the Bible to the middle, as close as you can. Where did you land? Of course, that depends upon the extra pages and helps a particular Bible may have. But let's assume we are just dealing with the Bible pages proper. The middle should be somewhere in the Psalms. To be precise, the middle of the KJV Bible would be Psalm 103. Now open that second half in half. That middle will fall somewhere near the beginning of the New Testament or the book of Matthew. Knowing this is a helpful skill for finding your way around the Bible.

Learning and memorizing the order of the books of the Bible will help a reader navigate the Bible. Few readers want to continually turn to the table of contents every time they look for a particular passage. Learning to find a passage quickly takes time and practice. Eventually, it becomes second nature.

Lesson Learned from Reading My Bible

Among the lessons I have learned, three top the list: First, reading in context matters. I can jump around and read a verse here and another verse there, but the more jumping I do, the less understanding I have. Secondly, if I really want to understand the Bible. I need to find out what it says rather than reading it to prove what I already think and believe. The difference between those two approaches matters. Finally, I have learned that Bible reading is really about transformation, not information. I read not just to learn old stories about ancient people. I read it because I want to know how to better serve the Creator who made me and loves me right now. The more I seek his will rather than read to find support for my will, the more I understand the Bible.

More than a history book, the Bible is a love letter from my Heavenly Father. It may not have always been written *to* me, but the more I understand it, the more I realize that it was written *for* me. The Holy Spirit uses that book to transform my life and point me toward the center of his will. Few other things in this world come even close to accomplishing that work in my life.

Understanding the significance of the Old Testament and the New Testament and their differences is vital. That's the next stop on our journey through the "greatest book ever written."

***

Going Deeper—Chapter 1

1.　When did you receive your very first Bible? What do you remember about the occasion? Why did you receive that Bible? Who gave it to you? Do you remember what translation it was? What ever happened to that first Bible?

2.　How much of the total Bible would you estimate you have read? Don't worry. How much Bible you have read is not a measure of your faith or spiritual life. How much you *want* to read might be! What parts have you read most? What parts have you left unread? Why?

3.　What translation of the Bible do you currently use? Why that particular version?

4.　When you first read the Bible on your own, where did you begin? What did you turn to first? Where would you recommend a new Bible reader begin?

5.　From your own personal perspective, why do you think reading and understanding the Bible is important?

Chapter 2: A Tale of Two Testaments

The first thing you will likely notice when you open your Bible for the first time is the fact that it is divided into an Old Testament and a New Testament. Understanding the difference will go a long way toward making your reading understandable.

Testament is a word not used in our everyday experiences. The biblical word translated as testament meant a covenant or a kind of contract. About the only place we use the term testament in our setting is in reference to a "last will and testament," the legal document containing the terms of a deceased's estate. The ancient Hebrew word for a covenant literally referred to a "cutting or dividing." Its meaning came from the practice of cutting or sacrificing an animal as part of ratifying a covenant.

The ancient word was used for two different kinds of agreements. One was similar to a contract. Two relatively equal parties negotiated, came to terms and finally agreed to the contract. Each agreed to certain responsibilities and the consequences for failing to meet those responsibilities. The second type of agreement refers to a legal agreement between two unequal parties. The greater party would offer the terms of the potential agreement. The lesser party would accept or reject the terms. No negotiations took place. The greater party offered; the lesser responded.

In the context of the Bible, God, the greater party, out of his grace and goodwill, offers to humans the lesser party, the terms of the covenant. The lesser believes, accepts, and then follows the terms of the covenant. God graciously offers; man believes and accepts, or not! Viewed through this lens of grace, God promises and the recipient believes. God is the promise-maker.

As we read the Bible, we can follow a chain of references to God's covenant-making (or testament-making) from beginning to end. The first is found in Genesis 6:18 and 9:10 in reference to God's promises to Noah before and after the flood. The Lord next initiates a covenant relationship with Abram, later named Abraham (Gen 9:9-17; 15:18; 17:1-21). In Exodus, the Lord "remembers" the promises to Abraham's family and intercedes on behalf of the Hebrew people enslaved in Egypt (Ex 2:24; 6:4-5). After the exodus from Egypt and at the foot of Mt. Sinai, the Lord again initiates a covenant with the people of Israel, which results in the Ten Commandments and all the regulations that would follow (Ex 19:5; 24:1-8).

Throughout the rest of the history of Israel, this original covenant remains the central focus of the faith, so much so that the crucial part of the Tabernacle and later the temple was termed—the Ark of the Covenant. The Ark and its Mercy Seat was the place where God and Israel met. In the Holy of Holies, the innermost sanctuary, atonement was made, promises remembered, and faith renewed. This was all part of the covenant. This covenant would remain the reference point for the Jewish faith throughout the rest of the Old Testament.

A New Covenant Promised

Toward the end of Old Testament history, we begin to hear a different voice. This one looked forward, not backward. Jeremiah, the prophet who witnessed the collapse of the Israelite nation, its capital, and, worst of all the temple, declared that a new and better day lay ahead. "The days are coming," declares the Lord. "When I will make a new covenant with the people of Israel and with the people of Judah. It will not be like the covenant I made with their ancestors when I took them by the hand to lead them out of Egypt, because they broke my covenant, though I was a husband to them," declares the Lord" (Jer 31:31-32). This "new" covenant would be new in kind as well as time. This also explains the Bible library's division into old and new testaments or covenants.

The New Testament continues this covenant talk. The Greek term for covenant is used four times in Matthew, Mark, and Luke, nine times in Paul's letters, twice in Acts, once in Revelation, and *seventeen* times in Hebrews!

Hebrews becomes the focus of a new understanding of the covenant and the fulfillment of Jeremiah's prediction that a new covenant was coming. The writer insists that Christ was the mediator of a new covenant (9:15). Hebrews further argues, "For if there had been nothing wrong with that first covenant, no place would have been sought for another" (8:7). The writer then cites Jeremiah's promise of a new covenant (8:8-12). He concludes by saying, "By calling this covenant "new," he has made the first one obsolete, and what is obsolete and outdated will soon disappear" (Heb 8:13).

The idea that the old was giving way to the new is not isolated to Hebrews. Jesus insisted that the Old Testament could not fail but it could end. He tells the legalistic-minded Pharisees, "The Law and the Prophets were proclaimed until John. Since that time, the good news of the kingdom of God is being preached, and everyone is forcing their way into it" (Lk 16:16). That word for "forcing" is only used twice in the New Testament and because of that is difficult to understand. It probably means that the news of the kingdom of Christ, in contrast to the oppression of the old message, is so refreshing that people were rushing to hear it. Jesus even used new covenant language at the Last Supper. "In the same way, after the supper, he took the cup, saying, "This cup is the new covenant in my blood, which is poured out for you" (Lk 22:20).

This was also the message of the Transfiguration of Jesus. Peter, James and John witnessed a vision of Jesus conversing with Moses and Elijah, the key figures of the Law and the Prophets. Together, they represented the entirety of the Old Testament. A voice from heaven announces, "This is my beloved son, with whom I am well pleased, listen to him" (Matt 17:5). These words formed a reprise of the announcement at Jesus's baptism. Here, the message is clear—Jesus is the one to be listened to now, not the Law or the Prophets.

Paul continued this theme in his letters. He insisted that something new had replaced the old. The old had served its purpose, but that purpose had been accomplished. "Before the coming of this faith," he told the Galatians believers who struggled with the status of the Jewish covenant now that Gentiles were coming to the Messiah, "We were held in custody under the law, locked up until the faith that was to come would be revealed" (3:23). "Until"—something changed with the coming of Christ. He goes on to explain, "So the law was our guardian until Christ came that we might be justified by faith. Now that this faith has come, we are no longer under a guardian" (24-25).

The old covenant paved the way for something new—the coming of the Messiah. Its mission had been accomplished. Under the old, Jew and Gentile were segregated. Under the new, they are united. "So in Christ Jesus, you are all children of God through faith, for all of you who were baptized into Christ have clothed yourselves with Christ. There is neither Jew nor Gentile, neither slave nor free, nor is there male and female, for you are all one in Christ Jesus. If you belong to Christ, then you are Abraham's seed, and heirs according to the promise" (26-29).

Paul says the new covenant, in contrast to the old, is of the spirit, not just the letter (2 Corinthians 3:6). He insists, "The letter kills, but the spirit gives life." He calls the old "the ministry of death carved in letters in stone" (3:7). He said the old was being brought to an end (3:11).

The Bible is divided into two main parts—the Old Testament and the New Testament. We might term them the Jewish Scriptures and the Christian Scriptures. Using covenant talk, we might term them the First Testament and the Last Testament or the Preliminary Testament and the Final Testament. The New has surpassed and replaced the Old. The Old didn't fail. It completed its task. It is finished. The New has come.

Do Christians Need the Old Testament?

This discussion raises a big question, one that has confounded believers for centuries—what is the place of the Old Testament for the follower of Jesus? To phrase it in even starker terms—do Christians need the Old Testament?

My answer: *it's complicated!* The question defies a simple yes OR no answer. I can only give a yes AND no answer. Let's explore this conundrum for a moment.

First, the yes. Yes, Christians need the Old Testament. The Old Testament is extremely helpful for the Christian to understand and fully appreciate the New Testament. The New references, quotes, alludes to, and offers many intentional parallels to the Old Testament. The Psalms, for example, provide valuable lessons on prayer and worship. The Old points to Jesus. After his resurrection, "beginning with Moses and with all the prophets, [Jesus] explained to them the things concerning Himself in all the Scriptures" (Lk 24:27). The Old Testament helps a believer understand Jesus' mission and message. As sages of old have said, "The old is the new concealed; the new is the old revealed." The two belong together. But this statement needs clarification.

Now, the no. Do Christians need the Old Testament? Let's be clear about this: Christians don't need the Old Testament to be right with God, in other words, to be saved. The Old Testament laws shed considerable light on God's standards of right and wrong, but these laws are totally incapable of providing the power or the will to live by those standards. Paul explains it this way, "But now, by dying to what once bound us, we have been released from the law so that we serve in the new way of the Spirit, and not in the old way of the written code." (Rom 7:6). Jesus' death on the cross as a sacrifice for sin is the only means of forgiveness before a holy and just God. The Old Testament can point us toward that truth, but it never explains or fully reveals that truth. That comes in the Gospel.

Do Christians need the Old Testament for our standard of right and wrong? Some argue that without the Old Testament and especially the Ten Commandments, we would be left without a rudder to guide us through the ethical currents of a godless world. The fact is the Ten Commandments were part of a covenant relationship between the Lord and the people of Israel. Gentiles were never held responsible for the tablets handed down at Mt. Sinai (See Rom 2:12-16). Christians live by a higher standard than the Ten Commandments. We are bound to the teachings of Jesus, who broadened and deepened the Old Testament standards (See Matt 5:21-48). To settle for the Ten Commandments is to settle for a lower standard. Do Christians need the Old Testament as the standard of right and wrong. The answer is NO!

Put simply, the Old Testament/Law had a three-fold purpose. First, it projected the character of God. Through its laws, principles, and history, we catch a glimpse of the heart and will of the Creator. At times, the picture is out of focus and distorted by the broken lives chronicled in the Old Testament, but the outline remains. Second, the covenant law, in particular, was intended to preserve the nation of Israel for God's purpose. The food laws, restrictions on association with idolatrous neighbors, and the many rituals about holiness and avoidance of contamination of all kinds were like a fence around a special people with a special calling. Finally, and most importantly, the whole of the Old Testament was designed to prepare for the coming of the Messiah. He was the goal. The law, the rituals, and the prophecies of the coming of a new covenant someday were all intended to point a spotlight on the One who would eventually come to bless the world.

The first of these purposes was carried over and amplified in the life and teaching of Jesus. The second and third were fully accomplished in Christ. Did the Old Testament/Covenant fail? Of course not! But it is fulfilled, completed, and finished in Christ. As Christians, we don't follow it. To try to live by it is to attempt to live in the past, to aim for a lower standard. Even that will not be met by anyone outside of the power of the Gospel and presence of the Holy Spirit.

The First Christians and the Old Testament Issue

The early years of the New Testament church provide an interesting example of believers struggling with this question. In the first few years of the church, Christians were nearly all people born and raised in the Old Testament. They were Jews who came to believe the message that Jesus was indeed the promised Messiah of the prophets. They gathered together to rehearse the message of Jesus, encourage one another in their newfound faith, and explore ways to spread the message of Jesus among their friends and neighbors. For the most part, they continued their Jewish way of life guided by the Old Testament and the traditions of their fore-fathers.

But everything changed when non-Jews, who knew nothing of the Old Testament, began to embrace the Gospel (Acts 11:1-26; 15:1-35). This new circumstance created controversy and raised a lot of questions the church had never had to face before. Can non-Jews become Christians without first becoming Jews? Can a person come to the Christ of the New Testament without first passing through the Old Testament? This was no small problem. Before this, no one had come to Christ without knowing and observing the Old Testament. Was that necessary? Must one accept the Old Testament precepts and practices before accepting the New Testament Gospel?

The story of how the apostles and the early church wrestled with those questions is recorded in Acts 15. Galatians and Romans explain the implications of their decision and provide guidance for how the churches should apply those decisions in future relationships between Jews and Gentile believers. It would remain complicated for years to come.

In the simplest of terms, their conclusion was this: Jews could continue to practice the Old Testament, its food laws, its way of life, and traditions if...! The "if" was important:

• If they didn't look down on others because they didn't follow the Old Testament way of life. The Gospel allowed no room for such pride or self-righteousness.

• If they didn't begin to think that observing the Law or the Jewish way of life was what made them right with God. Jew and Gentile alike were saved by grace through faith in what Christ had done for them on the cross and in the resurrection. To think that observing the Law saved a person was the same as saying the cross was unnecessary.

• If they didn't demand that others, especially non-Jews, follow the Old Testament way of life.

Keeping Jews and Non-Jews in the Same Church

But at the same time, certain expectations were placed on non-Jewish believers. The church's leaders deemed this necessary, most likely because of the stereotypical way Jews viewed Gentiles. This grew out of the Old Testament goal of preserving a people distinct and separate (holy) from the pagan nations around them. But over the years, this sense of separation had gone to seed. Many Jews were born and raised to see all Gentiles as 1) idol-worshipping pagans, 2) gluttons who ate all manner of nasty things, and 3) sexually promiscuous heathens who continually indulged in, or at least tolerated gross and indecent behavior. In many cases, this may have been partly true. But true or not, it was the lens through which Jews tended to view Gentiles.

This presented a problem. How could Jews and Gentiles who accepted Jesus as the Messiah and Lord of their lives come together in worship and fellowship as the church? The goal was one church, not a Jewish church and a separate Gentile church (Eph 2:11-22). Their solution was straightforward. Gentile believers must do all within their power to not further that negative stereotype.

The Jerusalem Council asked the Gentile Christians to do three things for the sake of Christian unity (Acts 15:28-29). 1) They were asked to stay away from anything that smacked of idolatry. 2) They should avoid foods that contain blood or otherwise insult the Jewish sensibilities about contaminated food. 3) No hint of sexual immorality should be tolerated among them. All these "asks" were directly related to the Jewish-Gentile stereotype and designed to foster fellowship between the two groups. These were not "salvation" issues; they were fellowship matters. Unity depended upon them.

Do Christians need the Old Testament or its laws? As I said, the answer is complicated. The real answer is Yes AND No.

The Best Treasure

Owning a Bible is a good thing. My first Bible changed my life. But just owning a Bible is not enough. Reading it is better. The more I read the Bible, the more I agree with the Psalmist. The Scriptures are "more precious than gold than much pure gold; they are sweeter than honey than honey from the honeycomb" (Ps 19:10). Understanding it is better yet. Recognizing why it contains two testaments has always been an important key to understanding its mysteries. But better even than understanding the Bible is believing in the Savior it tells me about and enjoying the life only he can make possible.

***

Going Deeper—Chapter 2

1. If a friend who didn't know much about the Bible asked you to explain the difference between the Old Testament and the New Testament, where would you begin? What would you say?

2. Do Christians need the Old Testament? Why or why not? Remember, it's complicated!

3. Read Acts 15:1-31. This was a critically important event in the life of the early church. Why was the meeting needed? What was the problem? What was the conclusion?

4. For practice finding your way around the Bible, see how quickly you can find the following passages: Acts 11:26; John 20:31; Isaiah 55:10-11; Deuteronomy 6:4; Ephesians 2:8-10.

Chapter 3: The Story of God

Imagine you have gone to the mall, a new mall, one that you have never been to before. It's a big. Perhaps, you have decided to visit the Mall of America in Minneapolis, the largest mall in North America. The Mall of America contains four floors, for a total of 5.6 million square feet. Its 520 stores, fifty restaurants, three hotels, a theme park complete with rollercoasters, and the 1.3 million gallon aquarium employ 13,000 workers. Inside the mall you will find 30,000 plants and 400 trees. Each year mall security returns 3,700 lost children to their parents. And I am sure you want to know that the mall also has 275 water efficient toilets for your shopping enjoyment! Did I mention that it's big?

Once you've parked in one of the 20,000 parking places and have finally walked through one of the malls too-many-to-count entrances, you face your biggest problem. Where to begin? You could just wander around and see the sites. But that won't work if you actually want to do some shopping.

I must confess I am not much of a shopper. I am a hunter. When I go to the mall, and I try to avoid it at all costs, I track my prey. I spot it. I bag it. I drag it to my truck and head for home. I am in and out in ten minutes. Mission accomplished!

But let's assume you have come to shop. Maybe, you first need to find a bathroom. Where do you start? Everyone knows the answer. You look for one of those directory kiosks with the diagram of the mall and the "you are here" star. You locate your destination and make your plan. Now you are ready to shop.

Now forget the mall. Imagine a Bible is dropped in your lap. It's a big book. In fact, it's a library of sixty-six books bound inside one cover. Together these books contain 1,189 chapters; 929 in the Old Testament and 260 in the New for a total of 23,145 verses. Where do you begin? How do you start? You could you wander around sight-seeing—a verse here, a story there, on to a totally different place. You might begin at the beginning, as you would most other books, and slog your way through. You can do that, but you will have a tough task ahead. You might get some benefit from your reading, but not nearly as much as you might if you actually understood how the Bible is laid out. What you really need is one of those mall kiosks with a "you are here" sign to help you find your way around. This is your lucky day!

In the next few pages, I will provide a "map" of the Bible that can help you figure out the lay of the land and plan your journey accordingly. From it, you will learn how the Bible's sixty-six books actually tell one amazing story from beginning to end. One Ultimate Author guided the forty some different contributors to pen an account of God's plan for man and where each of us fit into that amazing story.

But before we look at the directory of the Bible, it is important to clear up one common misconception. The Bible is not a story of great men and women. The Bible is the *Story of God!* The Bible is not the record of men and women pondering and searching for God and then writing down their conclusions and the history of their experiences. The Bible claims to be more than that. The Bible is God's revelation to man. The Living God reveals himself through history, through men and women, young and old, and ultimately through his own visit to planet earth in the person of Jesus Christ. That's the story of the Bible, God's story!

When we actually pay attention, we will realize that apart from Christ, the Bible contains no stories of great men or women. All of the men and women in the Bible are broken! Even the big names are marred by big sins. None are saints, if we mean by saints perfect sinless people without stains or scars. The record is just the opposite. Every story in the Bible reveals how a powerful, yet gracious and loving, God uses broken people to accomplish his purposes. Only when we see the work of God in the pages of the Bible will we experience its true power and beauty.

The Story of God revealed in the sixty-six books of the Bible divides into six parts. If we think of it as a book, it has six chapters; a play or drama, six acts. Their titles: Creation, Conflict, Covenant, Christ, Co-mission, and finally the Coronation! Let's briefly explore these six chapters in the Story of God.

Chapter One: Creation

The Bible opens with creation. "In the beginning God created the heavens and the earth" (Gen 1:1). In two fast moving chapters, Genesis records the Living God bringing the universe into existence. He spoke and it happened. "The universe was formed at God's command, so that what is seen was not made out of what is visible" (Heb 11:3). Genesis 1 outlines in thirty-one verses the appearance of everything from the light and land, the sun and the moon to fish in the sea, and the plants and animals of the earth.

The grand finale comes with the special creation of man, male and female, in the very image of God. Genesis 1 paints with a big brush. Genesis 2 tightens the focus and fills in the most important details of mankind's making, their relationship with the Creator and the rest of creation, and the bond between male and female. Their Maker blesses the two and gives them charge over all that he has made.

That's the first act of the Story of God. Four lessons stand out. First, this opening section emphasizes the fact that God made the world and all that exists. Genesis provides little information about how he did it. At times, he simply spoke and a part of creation appeared. At other times, he says, "Let the land produce vegetation." He tells the water to "teem with living creatures." On the sixth day, he orders the land to "produce living creatures." And it was so! How it happened is secondary. Who did it is what matters!

Secondly, nothing happened by chance. The creation was not an accident. The Maker did everything with purpose and design. What we call the laws of nature are really the results of the order and plan that nature's God built into all that he made. A third vital lesson— the creation is not God. He made it. It is a divine product, but nature is not divine. Worshipping the creation rather than the Creator always yields catastrophic consequences (Rom 1:18-25).

Finally, mankind is a special creation. Man and woman were made from the same stuff. They were made for each other. Together they were created for a close and personal relationship with God. No one but God alone can fill human life with the purpose and destiny for which it was made. As Augustine (AD 354-430) famously prayed, "You have made us and drawn us to yourself, and our heart is restless until it rests in you."[1]

Chapter Two: Conflict

If the Bible told us only part of the story, we would be left with a profound mystery. Genesis 1 ends with "God saw all that he had made, and it was very good." A few chapters later we read, "The Lord saw how great the wickedness of the human race had become on the earth, and that every inclination of the thoughts of the human heart was only evil all the time" (6:5). What happened? Genesis 3-11 explains not only what happened but also the terrible consequences that resulted from what theologians call "the fall."

The man and woman fell for the lies of the tempter. They turned from a life of trust and fellowship with God to the terror of knowing they were at odds with the very One who had made them. The result was a broken world. Conflict between God and man spread to conflict between man and wife, brother and brother, man and nature, and eventually tribe versus tribe, and cities and nation in conflict with everything around them.

Chapter two (*The Conflict*) overflows with meaning. What we call sin did not begin as simple disobedience. Behind the act of eating from a forbidden tree was the desire for independence from God. The tempter offered Eve the promise that she could make her own rules, live by her own standards. Once she possessed the "knowledge of good and evil," no longer would she be dependent on God's version of right and wrong. She would be like God! Adam was no innocent bystander. He was complicit in all that happened. Together they envisioned a future without God. Little did they know where this would lead.

As a result of that first decision, every offspring of man would be born "east of Eden." No one would be left unstained by sin. Everyone owns a heart of rebellion and independence. Without that intimacy with God and its access to the ultimate source of life (the tree of life), each child of Eve becomes the "walking dead." The grave is only a matter of time!

Want evidence that this really happened? That we live in sin-dominated world? Read the daily newspaper. Watch any television newscast. Examine your own heart. As Solzhenitsyna, the Russian novelist, famously observed in his classic *Gulag Archipelago*, "The line between good and evil runs not through states, nor between classes, nor between political parties either—but right through every human heart"[2] The verdict is in—all have sinned and fallen short of the glory of God (Rom 3:23). "The wages of sin is death" (Rom 6:23).

The sin-soaked chapters of Genesis ends with humans attempting to "make a name for themselves" (11:4). The plan—to build a tower with a top in the heavens. Did they think they could fashion their own God-less path to the heavens? Such arrogance! Such foolishness! Obviously, the plan failed. The Living God saw to that!

The very next chapter of Genesis begins another story. God himself initiates construction of a bridge from heaven to earth. Construction on the bridge will continue for another two thousand years. When finally complete, it will be called *The Gospel!*

Chapter Three: Covenant

Genesis 12 introduces the *Story of Israel*. We could call it the Big Story, only to be surpassed by the Biggest Story yet to come. The remainder of Genesis records the many ups and downs of a single family. But the story is not really about Abraham, Isaac, Jacob or his twelve sons. This is God's Story. The One who would later call himself "the God of Abraham, Isaac, and Jacob" initiates a covenant relationship with one particular man and his family. He would renew that covenant with each succeeding generation. He would bless them if they would trust his promises, something Adam and Eve proved unwilling to do. The issue has always been whether a person would "believe God," not simply believe that He exists (Gen 15:6).

In return, the Promise-maker offered a place, a posterity, and a plan. Bit by bit, the covenant-plan unfolded. The turning point arrived when God called Moses to lead the Hebrew people out of Egypt and to a "promised land." The Exodus, both the book and the event, marks the start of the *Story of Israel.* The God of their fathers makes a covenant with this special people at Mt. Sinai. The Ten Commandments, the rest of the Law, its rules and ceremonies, priesthood and tabernacle, all quickly follow. Warriors, kings, and mighty men and women of valor would follow—all people of the covenant. But Israel was a broken nation. It was led and made up of broken people. More often than not, Israel faltered and sometimes totally failed. But God remained good and gracious. His plan never stopped moving forward.

The entire Old Testament from Exodus through Malachi recounts the work of a faithful God working through unfaithful people. The plan would continue because it was never about this special people. It was always about a Person yet to come. He would be the seed of Eve, the future blessing promised to Abraham, a prophet like Moses. He would come from the tribe of Judah, a branch from the root of Jesse, a mighty king like David. This covenant was always forward-looking.

Eventually, the prophets would speak of a "new" covenant that would make the old obsolete (Jer 31:31; Heb 8:13). A glorious savior and servant would inaugurate this new promise. Through all the ups and downs of Israel, the covenant-making God channeled history forward toward the "fullness of time." All of the Old Testament—the Law and the Prophets—marched forward on a path that would lead directly to Bethlehem and the Christ, the Promised One. From the last page of Malachi, the finale of the Old Testament, we turn the page from the Big Story to the Biggest Story and the next chapter in the *Story of God*.

The *Story of God* begins with creation—the beginning of everything we know and see. Much would follow this beginning. Conflict and corruptions soon left the story stained and hardly recognizable. But God wasn't finished. The Story had barely begun. The next chapter would mark a decisive turning point. The Creator's offer of a covenant relationship with Abraham and his family sent the Story in a totally unexpected direction. But the *Story of God*, his self-revelation in history, was far from complete. In a sense, these first three chapters, which we know as the Old Testament, provide a preface or a preparation for the Biggest Story yet to come.

Chapter Four: Christ

The ancients said that "in the Old Testament, the New is concealed; in the New Testament, the Old is revealed." What was but a promise in the Old becomes reality in the New Testament. Others have said that the message of the Old Testament was, "Someone is coming!" The news of the New Testament is, "Someone has come!" Everything before Matthew was prelude. The most earth-shattering news ever imaginable was just about to be announced.

Years ago, I learned an unforgettable lesson about life and, of all things, helicopters. At the time, my oldest son was the "eye in the sky" reporter for a network television station in Atlanta. Since he had to work, I went to visit him on Christmas Eve at the small general aviation airport on the outskirts of the city where he waited a call from the station and his next assignment. While he was showing me around the airport, his pager sounded. He and his pilot were off to cover an incident on the expressway a few miles away. He offered to let me ride along. As the considerate parent that I am, I told him I didn't want to be in the way. He just smiled politely as he climbed aboard the chopper. He knew what I knew! His father gets dizzy on the second rung of a step ladder.

He returned an hour or so later and picked up the tour where we had left off. At one point, he stopped and pointed at the top of his helicopter and asked, "Dad, do you happen to know what they call that thing up there?" He was looking at an assortment of springs, fasteners, sprockets, and bolts that sat atop the big rotor blade. I didn't. He explained, "That last piece of hardware, the one on the very top, has a name. Everyone calls it by that name. The official repair manuals and the manufacturer's schematics all use the same terminology. That top piece is called 'the Jesus Nut.' My pilot tells me everyone calls it that because if that bolt ever fails, you better start talking to Jesus—fast. 'The Jesus Nut' holds the entire thing together."

That's true of the Bible as well! Jesus holds the whole thing together! He is the promised one of the Old Testament, the person who stands front and center in the Gospels, and the One the rest of the New Testament points back to and insists is coming again. Jesus is the Christ. His is the Biggest Story!

This *Story of Jesus* was also a surprising story. He was the promised Messiah of Israel. But He was not what most expected. He was more. He was God in flesh, the Creator taking the form of a man, living life in the midst of his creation. This chapter of the *Story of God* records Jesus' surprising teachings and his amazing miracles. He wasn't merely adding a footnote to the Old Testament. His life, ministry, and teachings completed everything to which the preceding three-fourths of the Bible were pointing. Without him, the rest were meaningless.

But even Jesus' miracles and teachings were not the main thing. Matthew, Mark, Luke, and John point the spotlight squarely on his atoning death, burial, and victorious resurrection. Those events become the heart of the Gospel. In fact, the writers of the four Gospels devote more space to the last week of Jesus' life than they do to any given year of his three year ministry. Later, Paul would insist, "For what I received I passed on to you as of first importance: that Christ died for our sins according to the Scriptures, that he was buried, that he was raised on the third day according to the Scriptures..." (1 Cor 15:3-4). The cross and resurrection stand at the heart of the Christian message. After his resurrection, Jesus spent forty days preparing his disciples for what would come next. Those final words to his disciples lead directly to the next chapter in the *Story of God*.

Chapter Five: The Co-Mission

With Chapter 4—Christ, the *Story of God* has reached a climactic turning point, but it is far from over. When Jesus ascended to heaven, he promised that the power and presence of the Holy Spirit would be with them (Acts 1:8; Matt 28:18-20). He commissioned them to spread the news of his victory over sin and death. The world became their mission field. No longer a Jew-only enterprise, the new community of believers they would gather was to include Jew and Gentile. Anyone and everyone, no matter their past, their class, race, nationality, status, wealth or lack thereof, would be welcome in the people of God. The one condition: everyone must acknowledge that he or she is a sinner who needs what Jesus offers and is ready to follow him and his teachings. This was the message and task Jesus gave his disciples.

Most importantly, they needed to understand that theirs was a *co-mission*. He was not abandoning them. They were not on their own. He, through the Holy Spirit, would continue to guide and direct them. The task was too big for human effort alone. They would need heaven's help. And that was exactly what they would receive!

Fifty days after the resurrection, Jesus kept his word. Earlier he had promised, "Let anyone who is thirsty come to me and drink. Whoever believes in me, as Scripture has said, rivers of living water will flow from within them." John explained, "By this he meant the Spirit, whom those who believed in him were later to receive. Up to that time the Spirit had not been given, since Jesus had not yet been glorified" (Jn 7:37-39). The promise became reality on the Day of Pentecost. The Spirit came. The apostles proclaimed the *Story of Jesus*. Thousands joined this new work of God. The church was born! The church, then and now, is not just a human organization powered by all the ingenuity and strength that its members can muster. Christ's church is a Spirited-powered organism!

The newborn church struggled with more than a few birth pains. Those first Christians faced opposition from the outside and disagreements on the inside. Bit by bit, they grew in numbers and in an understanding of their task. The message of Jesus spread from Jerusalem to the villages of Judea, across the barrier of bigotry to Samaria, and then from synagogue to synagogue in the far flung regions of the empire. Eventually they told their story to non-Jews.

Luke records how, "Men from Cyprus and Cyrene, went to Antioch and began to speak to Greeks also, telling them the good news about the Lord Jesus. The Lord's hand was with them, and a great number of people believed and turned to the Lord" (Acts 11:20-21). These courageous Gospel pioneers were the first to bear the name "Christian" (Acts 11:26). Person by person, city by city, the mission advanced. It is still advancing wherever a follower of Jesus proclaims, lives, and shares the Gospel!

We all live in the *Co-mission* chapter of the *Story of God*. But one day, this chapter will end. Only the Lord will decide when and how. But at some point in the near or distant future, he will turn the page and we will enter the final chapter of his story.

Chapter Six: The Coronation

To be honest, I struggled for some time to find just the right word to describe this chapter in the *Story of God*. I knew the contents of the chapter, but I couldn't find the right term to describe it. I thought about *conclusion.* This is the Bible's last chapter in the *Story of God*, but somehow that didn't seem dramatic enough. I tried *consummation* for a while. That carried the right idea. God will one day hang a "closed for business" sign on his universe. This life as we know will come to a screeching halt, and the new heaven and the earth, the believer's eternal home, will commence. For a while, I toyed with the word *commencement.* This will be the beginning of a New Heaven and New Earth. But the more I pondered this word and discussed it with others, invariably our attention turned to our future reward. We talked about such things as streets of gold, the glories of our "mansions," and all the joy we will share with loved ones long since gone. Almost all of our talk of "last things" quickly turned inward. Finally, it occurred to me that our preoccupation with "us" misses the point of this last chapter of the *Story of God*.

I began to realize that maybe we have it all backwards. Perhaps our focus should be on him who has made it all possible, the one who loved us when we didn't deserve it and through every step of our journey of faith. The last chapter of the *Story of God* is about *him*. Our Lord is coming again! Every eye shall behold him. "For the Lord himself will come down from heaven, with a loud command, with the voice of the archangel and with the trumpet call of God, and the dead in Christ will rise first. After that, we who are still alive and are left will be caught up together with them in the clouds to meet the Lord in the air. And so we will be with the Lord forever" (1 Thes 4:16-18). With the Lord forever!

The final chapter is about far more than our reward. The Bible's *Story of God* ends with the coronation of the universe's rightful monarch. For the first time, we will see him as he is, in all of his glory and beauty. "Every knee will bow and every tongue confess that he is Lord" (Phil 2:11). He will be crowned King of kings and Lord of lords. We will be honored guests at the great celebration of the Wedding Feast of the Lamb. Who is the center of attention at a wedding? It is certainly not the guests! The ultimate finale to the story of the Bible is the crowning of King Jesus.

Interestingly, the Bible ends very much as it began. A new creation replaces the scarred and soiled original. A new garden paradise appears with a Tree of Life at its center. Once again, everyone in the new heaven and the earth will live in full fellowship with Almighty God (Rev 22:1-5). Heaven is only heaven because he is there!

Much about the future the Lord has in store for his people is on a "need to know basis." A few things are clear. This world has an end-date. We just don't know when. The believer's task remains—to prepare for the long haul, but live as if the end could be tomorrow. We don't know the Lord's timetable. Speculation and date-setting leads to nowhere good. We know this for sure—those in Christ can look forward to a blessed future; those who don't, not so much. The Living God will be both fair and just. Come, Lord Jesus, come!

***

This is the Story of God. Our Lord has revealed his plan in these six chapters—Creation, Conflict, Covenant, Christ, Co-mission, and finally the Coronation. Together these chapters tell where we have been, what he desires of us here and now, and where he is taking us in the future. With this outline of the Bible in mind, you can open the book and find the "you are here" star. From there, you can calculate your starting point. You will know what part of the story has gone before and what will follow. No longer will you need to wander around the Bible like a stranger in the mall.

***

Going Deeper—Chapter 3

1. Open your Bible to the table of contents page. Read through the list of the books of the Bible. Practice pronouncing the names. If you have difficulty, some Bible dictionaries and most digital Bibles will offer pronunciation help. This might be a good time to start memorizing the order of the books. See how many you can memorize within the next week.

2. Just for fun, what's the biggest book, other than the Bible, that you have read or attempted to read? How successful were you?

3. According to *Navigating*, who is the main character of the Bible? Why is it important to remember this when reading or studying the Bible?

4. The *Story of God* is divided into six sections or chapters. Name the six chapters in order and give a two or three-sentence description of each.

5. Where do you live in this timeline of the *Story of God*? Why is this important?

Chapter 4: Lessons from the Library

The Bible is a big and varied book. It is so big that it might more properly be called a library. It contains sixty-six books, thirty-nine of those books are in the Old Testament. The Old Testament alone would probably be the biggest book many of us would ever attempt to read. Because of its sheer size, even veteran readers can get lost.

Some of the Old Testament books are big books in themselves. One single chapter in the Psalms (119) could swallow several of the other books whole, with room left over. A few books are tiny by comparison, just a few short chapters. The complete book of Obadiah consists of just twenty-one verses. Some books include strange mysteries and visions. Others contain what we would consider weird and archaic rules. Most readers are drawn to the exciting tales of intrigue and adventure found in some. A lot of us get lost in the deserts of Leviticus. The Bible is a big book!

But it is God's book for us. Reading it, and better yet, knowing it, always proves well worth the effort. Anyone who devotes effort and time to exploring its treasures will be richly rewarded. The Bible offers a lifetime of discovery and growth. St. Jerome (fourth century AD) put it like this, "The Scriptures are shallow enough for a babe to come and drink without fear of drowning and deep enough for theologians to swim in without ever touching the bottom."

Before we begin our exploration of the Old Testament library, we need to first consider a few important preliminaries. These will prove beneficial on our journey.

The Most Important Unknown Verse

First, let's pause and reflect on one of the least known and yet most important verses in the Old Testament. I refer to Deuteronomy 29:29. First, consider the context. In Deuteronomy, Moses reviews the covenant with the new generation just before they enter the Promised Land. Their parents had forfeited the right to enter the land by their refusal to trust the Lord (Nm 13-14). Now, forty years later, Moses prepares the children of that lost generation to go where their parents wouldn't. Moses concludes the review and pauses before he calls the new generation to commit themselves to the covenant and the challenge ahead.

This call to commitment comes in Deuteronomy 30 with the choice of "life or death" (30:11-20). Moses, now an older man, offers his parting words, chooses his successor (Joshua), and disappears into the wilderness to die (Dt 31-34). After outlining the covenant and calling for their commitment, Moses interjects this little verse. It seems abrupt and almost out of place. Yet, Deuteronomy 29:29 provides a critical reminder about how any believer, then or now, must approach the Word of God. It reads, "The secret things belong to the Lord our God, but the things revealed belong to us and to our children forever, that we may follow all the words of this law."

This verse offers some important lessons that we need as we approach the Old Testament. First, God's plans are on a need-to-know basis. He has not told us everything, just what we need to know. Our task is to concentrate on what he has revealed. God knows more than we do and always will (Isa 55:8-9). We need to accept that fact. Adam and Eve didn't. Their quest to know what God alone knew proved fatal for all of us. Secondly, speculating about the secret things, what God has not revealed, will always prove an unprofitable task (2 Tim 2:14-16). Third, what we don't know should never become an excuse for disobeying what we do know. Mark Twain hit on an important truth when he reportedly noted, "It ain't the parts of the Bible that I can't understand that bother me. It is the parts that I do understand." Our challenge is to act on what God has revealed and not waste time speculating about what he hasn't.

Finally, as you read the Old Testament, expect to not understand some things. I guarantee you will encounter passages that will confuse you. A few of the Old Testament laws and even some of the events will seem strange and bewildering. You may likely find particular passages that are difficult to square with the teachings of Jesus. Don't let those passages stop you. Keep reading. Put a question mark beside the passage or begin a separate list of difficult passages for later study. You will find many answers to your questions simply by continuing to read. Whether your questions persist or not, don't let the questions become an excuse for not reading further. Persistence will be rewarded!

Those Extra Books

Two more preliminaries before we begin our exploration of the Old Testament library. First, at some point, you will likely discover that the Roman Catholic Old Testament has fourteen books not found in most Protestant Bibles. What about these "apocryphal" or hidden books? It's complicated, but the short answer is this. These additional books were never considered part of Hebrew Scripture by the Jewish rabbis. Hebrew scholars looked upon these books as the kind of literature that a faithful Jew would profit by reading even though they were not God's Word. They viewed them like many Christians might view *Pilgrims's Progress, Paradise Lost,* or *the Confessions of St. Augustine.* Despite the fact that the books were never considered

Scripture, the Roman Catholic Council of Trent (1545-63 AD) made them a test of faithfulness to the church. The council declared that anyone who refused to recognize the fourteen books would be considered a heretic by the church. The decision was as much a political power play as it was religious guidance.

Nonetheless, the books are worth reading. A few contain additions to some of the original Hebrew books. Most attempt to fill in the blanks around the four hundred years between the end of the Old Testament and the beginning of the New. Humans don't like vacuums. Someone will always attempt to fill the silence. The most interesting book (The Maccabees) relates the stories of the Jewish fight for independence in the second century BC. The rebels managed to temporarily wrestle control of Jerusalem and the Jewish temple from the Greek military. The Jewish militants cleansed the temple and rededicated it to the worship of Yahweh, following the many abominations performed in the sanctuary by the pagans. The Jewish Feast of Lights, or Hanukkah, commemorates these events.

It is helpful to also note that the English Bible is organized differently than the Hebrew Bible. Recognizing this will prevent some confusion when you come across references to the structure of the Hebrew Bible in the New Testament. Note Luke 24:44, "He [Jesus] said to them, "This is what I told you while I was still with you: Everything must be fulfilled that is written about me in the Law of Moses, the Prophets and the Psalms." The Hebrew Bible was divided into these three categories. The Law or Torah, sometimes simply referred to as the Books of Moses, included Genesis through Deuteronomy. The Prophets contained twenty-one books, most of what the English Bible calls the history books, plus the Major Prophets. The rest fell into the category of The Writings, sometimes simply referred to as the Psalms, because that book was considered the principal book. The Prophets were nicknamed simply Isaiah for the same reason. Don't be confused by any references to these categories. The contents remain the same as the English Bible.

The Combination that Unlocks the Old Testament Library

Now, we are ready to stroll through the Old Testament library. Libraries can be organized in lots of different ways. Many literal libraries follow the Dewey Decimal System. Others organize at least part of their collections according to the Library of Congress System. The oldest part of the Trinity College library in Dublin, Ireland, shelved books by size: tall books on one shelf, shorter ones on another. Most of us follow some simplified combination of these systems in our personal collections of books. We sort some books by topic, some by authors, others by size, and perhaps part of our collection simply by the color of the covers. Knowing how a particular library is organized prevents a great deal of wasted time and energy.

Let me give you the combination that will unlock the door to this library of thirty-nine books: 5-12-5-5-12. The Old Testament library is divided into five sections: five books of Law, twelve books of History, five books of Poetry, five Major Prophets, and twelve Minor Prophets. This might be a good time to open your Bible to the Table of Contents.

The five books of Law mirror the Torah of the Hebrew Bible. Genesis, which means beginnings, tells the story of creation and the events that led to the birth of Israel. Exodus gets its name from the major event that leads to the rest of the *Story of Israel* and is memorialized each year in the Jewish Passover celebration. Numbers recounts the census taken in preparation for the initial conquest of the Promised Land. When the Hebrew people refused to cross into the land, an entire generation was sentenced to wander in the wilderness for forty years. Much of Numbers summarizes the key events of these forty years. Leviticus, named for the priestly tribe of Levi, details the many laws regarding the Jewish priesthood, sacrifices, related purity laws, and the ceremonies of the Tabernacle. Deuteronomy, a title that means second law, contains Moses's review of the covenant for the second generation of Israelites as they prepared to enter the Promised Land, this time without Moses.

The twelve books of History tell the story of the conquest of Canaan, the tumultuous years that followed, and the rise and fall of the Jewish kingdom. The history covers a period of roughly a thousand years. We will look more closely at the details in the next chapter. Two particular notes of interest: 1 and 2 Chronicles repeat much of the story previously told in the books of Samuel and Kings. Chronicles, however, spotlights the events related to the priesthood and the temple. The story is much the same. The focus differs. Another important note: everything in the remaining twenty-two books fits back into the historical events recorded in the first seventeen. Sometimes, we are given clues that tell where they fit, sometimes not.

What Makes Poetry Poetry

The next shelf in the Old Testament library holds five books of poetry—Job through Song of Solomon. The contents are rich and varied. The Psalms provide an amazing resource for personal and corporate worship. Proverbs offers a collection of Hebrew wisdom literature. This "wisdom" combines revealed insights and common sense observations on life. The Song of Solomon provides the closest thing to a romance poem in the Bible. In poetic verse, it follows the growing love between a prince and a common village maiden. In Ecclesiastes, Solomon reflects on the meaning of life and the many false paths that can distract from true fulfillment. Job offers a classic exploration of why good people suffer and how God fits into such experiences. All of these are written with imagination and poetic flair.

Of particular importance is an understanding of Hebrew poetry. Three characteristics stand out:

First, like all poetry, these works most often target the heart rather than the head. They tug at the emotions. It's not that they are not rational or logical. They can be, but that's not the primary emphasis. Both content and form aim at the heart.

Secondly, as with almost all poetry, the writers flood their works with non-literal language. They seek to touch the imagination with metaphors, word pictures, analogies, and idealized descriptions. For example, a writer of prose may speak of God's care and provision. The poet would make the same appeal with words such as, "The Lord is my shepherd, I lack nothing. He makes me lie down in green pastures, he leads me beside quiet waters, he refreshes my soul." (Ps 23:1-3). Both describe the same truth.

When the Old Testament prophets spoke of God's judgment, they often described it poetically. Joel 1, for example, describes an invasion of locusts. In the next chapter, Joel paints a word picture of the pending judgement of God. He pictures the judgement as if it were a locust plague devouring the land. Ezekiel 37 describes a valley of dry bones coming to life. The prophet was actually proclaiming the revival that the Spirit of the Lord could bring to the wayward people of Israel. Recognizing the difference between literal and poetic languages can prevent a great deal of confusion. It is also important to note that Hebrew poetry is not limited to these five books of poetry. As noted, many of the oracles of the prophets came in poetic form.

Finally, Hebrew poetry is characterized by its use of pattern or rhythm. Simple English poetry, like that of nursery rhymes and many popular poems, follows a pattern of rhymes and sounds. Hebrew poetry seldom does. More often, the Psalms, for example, use a pattern of repetition or contrast. Psalm 106 offers an example of repetition, "Praise the Lord. Give thanks to the Lord, for he is good; his love endures forever. Who can proclaim the mighty acts of the Lord or fully declare his praise? Blessed are those who act justly, who always do what is right." The first line of each verse makes a statement; the second line repeats the same idea in different words. In other psalms, the second line contrasts with the first, or in other cases, the second builds on first verse. The possibilities are endless.

Psalm 119, the longest chapter in the Bible, provides another interesting example of Hebrew poetry. The 176 verses are organized into twenty-two stanzas of eight verses each. Why twenty-two? Because the Hebrew alphabet contained twenty-two letters! Each of the eight verses in each stanza begins with the same Hebrew letter. The first eight all begin with Aleph, the second eight with Beth, the third with Gimel, the fourth with Daleth, and so on through the entire Hebrew alphabet. Other examples, among many, of a similar alphabetic pattern include Psalm 9 and Psalm 10 together, Psalm 25, part of Lamentations, and Proverbs 31:10-31. The devotion and imagination required to create such works is astounding.

Most English Bibles print poetry in a different format than prose. For example, in my NIV Bible, Daniel 7:1-8 is printed in block form as prose. Verses 9-10 are indented and staggered to indicate a poetic form. Most Bibles follow this or a similar system to help distinguish one type of literature from the other. The categories, however, are not infallible. Sometimes, the context and personal judgment must be used to determine if a passage is prose or poetry.

Fore-telling and Forth-telling

The last two divisions of the Old Testament library both fall under the heading of prophecy. Our English language, however, presents a problem. For English, prophecy means fore-telling the future in some fashion. The biblical term differs. Both the Old Testament Hebrew and the New Testament Greek words for prophecy mean primarily forth-telling a message from God, which can include a measure of foretelling the future, but the foretelling is seldom the main thing. Most often, future predictions involve general statements of divine judgment or blessing. But sometimes, the prophet does provide precise predictions of future events.

In general, Old Testament prophets fell into two categories—those who committed their works to writing and those who didn't. Of course, the Old Testament prophets whose books bear their names all fall into the former group. Non-writing prophets would include men like Elijah, Elisha, Nathan, and others. After the division of Israel following Solomon's reign, some of the prophets ministered in the southern kingdom of Judah and others in the northern realm of Israel. A few carried God's message to a neighboring nation. Most of the time, the contents of the book make this clear.

English Bibles customarily divide the seventeen books of prophecy into two categories: Major Prophets and Minor Prophets. The primary distinction is the length of the books or, in the case of the original works, the size of the scrolls. While the Major Prophets each play major roles in the history of Israel, the label "minor" doesn't mean some of these other prophets were not important in their own right. Major and minor simply refer to the length of the works.

The main message of the prophets, major and minor, can be summarized as follows: 1) God has blessed the nation. 2) But the nation has been unfaithful to God in many ways. The most common complaints of the prophets focused on idolatry or injustice toward the poor. 3) Return to God and be blessed. 4) Don't return to God and face judgment. 5) But whether you return to God or not, He will be faithful to his covenant. His eternal plan will continue. You can only determine your part in that plan.

Jesus Fulfills the Old Testament

Jesus fulfills Old Testament prophesy. The prophets spoke of his birth, his life and influence, his death, and his resurrection. They explained the purpose of his coming and the necessity of his death for sin. They speak also of his future glory. In fact, Jesus himself insisted that the Old Testament prophets spoke of him (Lk 24:27). On resurrection Sunday, he told his disciples, "This is what I told you while I was still with you: Everything must be fulfilled that is written about me in the Law of Moses, the Prophets and the Psalms" (Lk 24:44).

Previously, Jesus had criticized the Jewish scholars for searching the Scriptures to find eternal life. That was a futile quest, he declared, because eternal life was not found in the Scriptures, but in him to whom the Scriptures pointed (Jn 5:39). Paul emphasizes the same truth when he writes that the Old Testament law led us to Christ and Christ now replaces the need for that law (Gal 3:23-24). Paul would later insist that his fellow Jews did not and could not understand the Scriptures until they began to read through the lens of the gospel of Jesus (2 Cor 3:13-16).

The Old Testament looks forward to the life and ministry of Jesus in a variety of ways. Sometimes, an Old Testament passage predicts a specific event in Jesus' life. At other times, the New Testament points to patterns in the Old Testament that are also present in Jesus' life. Sometimes, the New Testament highlights principles of the Old Testament that are found in Jesus' ministry. In other instances, the New Testament uses the Old Testament to illustrate and explain what is happening in Jesus' life and teachings. Jesus did not just fulfill Old Testament predictions; he completed the very purpose of these thirty-nine books.

***

That's the Old Testament library—thirty-nine books filled with adventure, inspiration, and glimpses into the very heart of God. The books are old—all over two thousand years old; some penned as much as thirty-five hundred years ago. Yet, they still contain the wisdom and revelation of the Living God. These very books still do what the Apostle Paul claimed when he insisted that the Holy Scriptures "are able to make you wise for salvation through faith in Christ Jesus. All Scripture is God-breathed and is useful for teaching, rebuking, correcting and training in righteousness, so that the servant of God may be thoroughly equipped for every good work" (2 Tim 3:15-17).

Next, we will look more closely at the history recorded in the Old Testament. We will focus on the Big Story, the startling account of how the Living God chose one family that would become a nation through which God would bless the whole world. As amazing as that story may seem, it pales in comparison to what would follow later—the Biggest Story of all!

***

Going Deeper—Chapter 4

1. Starting with Genesis, how many of the books of the Old Testament can you name in order? Make it your goal to be able to recite the entire list by a week from today.

2. Find Deuteronomy 29:29. What is the significance of this verse?

3. What is the explanation for most "Protestant" Bibles not including the added books found in the "Catholic" Bible?

4. What are the main divisions of the Old Testament library? Briefly summarize what is found in each.

5. What makes poetry? Why is this important for understanding the poetic sections of the Bible?

6. Why do you think the Old Testament matters to New Testament Christians?

Chapter 5: The Big Story

The Old Testament library consists of thirty-nine books covering well over two thousand years of history, but it contains one story. Everything in those thirty-nine books chronicles, illuminates, or illustrates the single storyline that runs from beginning to end. Our challenge is to keep that storyline in view. It's easy to lose ourselves in the details of the political events, the great literature, or the poetry. The story overshadows all of the individual pieces.

The Big Story—The *Story of Israel*

The Old Testament story was, and still is, a BIG Story. It records earthshaking events. Events so big that many find it hard to wrap their minds around it. This is BIG news! But, and this is important, the Old Testament message is not the BIGGEST news. The best is yet to come!

So, what's the BIG news of the Old Testament? It is this—the Living God, the creator of all that exists, reached down into history and chose one particular nation to be the vehicle of his blessing for the world. Moses explains this in his retelling of Hebrew history to the second generation after the Exodus:

"Ask now about the former days, long before your time, from the day God created human beings on the earth; ask from one end of the heavens to the other. Has anything so great as this ever happened, or has anything like it ever been heard of? Has any other people heard the voice of God speaking out of fire, as you have, and lived? Has any god ever tried to take for himself one nation out of another nation, by testings, by signs and wonders, by war, by a mighty hand and an outstretched arm, or by great and awesome deeds, like all the things the Lord your God did for you in Egypt before your very eyes?" (Dt 4:32-34).

The story of the Old Testament is the *Story of Israel*—how the God of heaven chose one people for his very own and slowly but faithfully began to unfold his plan for history through that nation. All of the Old Testament is about that Story. Unfortunately, Israel often misinterpreted its history. Some thought God had chosen them because they were better than other nations. Moses attempted to preempt that wrongheaded conclusion. Just before the second generation prepared to enter the Promised Land, he warned them, "Do not say to yourself, 'The Lord has brought me here to take possession of this land because of my righteousness.' …Understand, then, that it is not because of your righteousness that the Lord your God is giving you this good land to possess, for you are a stiff-necked people" (Dt 9:4-6). With this in mind, we are ready to look at the *Story of Israel* and how that story unfolds in the pages of the Old Testament library.

Where the *Story of Israel* Begins

This Big Story starts with a big event, so big that the rest of the story will point back to it again and again. This event would be memorialized in a weeklong annual celebration so that each generation would learn about it from the previous and never forget the big event that started it all. In many ways, this commemoration and its recalling of the events surrounding the Exodus was the high point of the Hebrew faith. The *Story of Israel* begins with the Exodus and the events surrounding it, as told in the second book of the Old Testament. If the story begins with the second book, what do we do with the first book? Recognizing the relationship of Genesis and Exodus is an important part of understanding how the Old Testament works.

The fifty chapters of Genesis relate to the *Story of Israel* in two different ways. The first eleven chapters serve as the *preface* to the story. Chapters 12-50 provide the *introduction*. A survey of these two literary parts will prepare us for a look at the *Story of Israel* itself.

The Preface to the *Story of Israel*

The preface to a book can function in different ways. The author can explain why she is writing the book. She can relate events that led to the story. Sometimes, the writer's preface can outline some things she thinks the reader might need to know before beginning the story. Or, as in the case of Genesis 1-11, the preface explains the reason for the *Story of Israel* and outlines the concepts that will help the reader make sense of the story that consumes the rest of the Old Testament library.

Genesis 1-11, as we have already noted in the chapter on the Story of God, relates the account of creation and the subsequent conflict that soon followed as a result of Adam and Eve's disobedience. The Almighty fashioned the universe and all that is in it. We can wonder about the whens, the whys, the hows, and countless other questions about creation that Genesis doesn't answer. We are told what we need to know to understand the story that will follow. God made the world. He created into it order and design. Everything about it was good. Mankind, male and female, were a special creation. Together, they were made by God and for God. The creator placed the two in an ideal place and walked with them in perfect fellowship.

All was good until it wasn't! Whatever else the account in Genesis 3 implies, this preface tells us that this original sin came in the form of doubt, distrust, and disobedience. The pair were tempted to doubt what they had been told. This led to a distrust of their Maker's motives. Distrust quickly deteriorated into disobedience to the one command they were forbidden to breach. Just as important as the nature of their sin were the consequences that followed. Without access to their source of life, the couple began a slow but inevitable march toward death. Their relationship with God was broken. How could they walk in fellowship with one they no longer trusted?

Before their own death, Adam and Eve were forced to watch helplessly as one son killed another. This first couple faced the unimaginable guilt of knowing what they had unleashed. The Genesis 1-11 preface leaves many questions unanswered, but what it tell us matters. Evil never stands still. It spreads and metastasizes. Nothing is spared. The "good" of Genesis 2:31 gives way to the total corruption of Genesis 6:5-6. What was once good turns into wickedness so great that the Lord regrets what he had made. Despite the fresh beginning after The Flood, the brokenness remained (Gn 9:15-28).

Genesis 4-11 chronicles the horrible story of a world spiraling from bad to worse. Corruption spreads from marriage to family, from cities and to whole civilizations. Everything becomes tainted and broken. A few call out to God. Others attempt to bridge their estrangement from God with a tower designed to reach the heavens. The Creator foils the effort. He has a better plan.

Genesis 12-50: The Introduction to the *Story of Israel*

Genesis 12 marks a new beginning in the record. We are still not to the story. In Genesis 12-50, the writer outlines the backstory. The story begins with the deliverance of the Hebrew people from slavery in Egypt. This introduction explains how the descendants of Abraham, Isaac, and Jacob found themselves in such a predicament.

Genesis 12-50 chronicles the stories of four generations of one family. It begins with the Lord's call of Abram. God promises a place, a progeny, and the promise that his family would become a blessing to the whole world. Abram responds in faith. He leaves his home in Ur, travels west toward an unknown land, and awaits the fulfillment of the Lord's promise of a family.

After numerous ups and downs, detours and discouragements, Abraham and Sarah have a long-awaited son, Isaac. Eventually, Isaac would become the father of twins Jacob and Esau. The younger of the twins, Jacob, rather than the firstborn Esau, was destined to carry the promise forward. An unlikely candidate to serve God's purposes, Jacob, the deceiver, "wrestles" with his Maker in more ways than one. He is eventually transformed into Israel, the man of God.

Jacob, now Israel, bears twelve sons. Their names would go down in the annals of Hebrew history as the twelve tribes of Israel. But the sons' stories are scarred by sibling rivalry. Joseph, then the youngest and the most favored, is sold into slavery by his jealous older brothers, who lie to their distraught father. They tell him that his beloved son has been killed by a wild animal. Little did the grief-stricken family know that the Lord was at work preparing for the next chapter in the story.

Joseph ends up in Egypt, where he rises through the ranks from slave to prince. Through the providence of God, Joseph guides Egypt through feast and famine. When Jacob sends his sons to Egypt to purchase food for his famished family, the last person they expect to encounter is their long-lost brother. After weeks of intrigue, fear, and finally unexpected surprises, Joseph reveals his identity and brings his family to Egypt, where he provides protection and provision. But eventually, Joseph died and with him, the fortunes of the Hebrew people. On the very next page, the story begins!

The *Story of Israel* in Eight Chapters

The *Story of Israel* begins with the opening pages of the book of Exodus. The preliminaries have been explained in Genesis 1-11. Genesis 12-15 tells the backstory—how Israel arrived at this desperate point. Now, we are ready to learn how the Lord "by his mighty hand and outstretched arm," created a chosen nation out of a huddled mass of terrified slaves. The *Story of Israel* becomes a major chapter in the *Story of God*.

<u>**The Birth of the Nation**</u>. The books of Exodus, Leviticus, Numbers and Deuteronomy recount the early history of Israel. Through signs and wonders, Moses leads his people out of Egypt and toward the Promised Land. The hasty exit from Egypt would provide the name to the second book of the Old Testament library and the occasion memorialized in the most cherished Jewish celebration—the Passover.

After a miraculous crossing of the Red Sea, the Lord directs the multitude by fire and cloud to the foot of Mt. Sinai. There, he inaugurates his covenant with his chosen people. The Ten Commandments and the many regulations that follow are recorded in the book of Exodus. Leviticus, named for the priestly tribe of Levi, contains the special practices and procedures that would accompany the Tabernacle, the many priestly sacrifices, and special purity rules for the new nation. God intends Israel to be a holy nation as well as a chosen people.

Numbers tell the story of the census of the twelve tribes in preparation for the invasion of the Promised Land. Out of fear, the nation refuses to move forward. As a result of their failure of faith, the Lord turned the people back toward the wilderness from which they had come. For forty years, an entire generation would wander and die in the desert. The Lord would offer the next generation the opportunity to make the Promised Land their own. The last half of Numbers summarizes the ups and downs of those forty lost years.

Deuteronomy, a term meaning second law, chronicles the preparation of the second generation of Israel to enter the Promised Land. Moses reviews the covenant to which the previous generation had committed themselves. Forbidden to enter the land himself, Moses bids farewell to his people, anoints Joshua as his successor, and disappears to his death. Thus ends the first section of the Old Testament library and the initial chapter of the Big Story.

<u>**The Conquest.**</u> The books of Joshua, Judges, and Ruth contain the account of the initial conquest of the Promise Land. Stories of defeat and victory, cowardice and bravery, along with the accompanying heroes and heroines, fill the pages. The battle for control of the land would prove difficult. The Lord was faithful; often, Israel was not.

Eventually, the land is divided among the tribes who settle their assigned territories. But pockets of resistance remain. For a few hundred years, the tribes confronted incursions from surrounding enemies bent on taking advantage of the fledgling nation. The Lord would raise up a hero after hero to defend one part of Israel or another. Nonetheless, a spirit of rebellion and disobedience reigns in Israel. That's the story of Judges.

As the chaos continues in the land, the book of Ruth offers a brief calm. Ruth tells the adventures of an immigrant widow who follows her Hebrew mother-in-law back to Israel. She is protected and eventually married by Boaz, a relative of her deceased husband. This romantic interlude provides the backstory to the next epoch in the *Story of Israel*. Ruth will become the great-grandmother of Israel's most celebrated monarch—King David.

<u>The Kingdom</u>. Tired of fighting isolated and fragmented battles against more powerful neighbors, the tribes of Israel cry out for a king to unite them and prepare them for battle, just like the other nations. The prophet Samuel warns that any future king would tax the people to enrich himself and draft their sons to fight wars against their will. But the nation persists. Israel anointed its first king—Saul. Tall and handsome, Saul looks the part and quickly rallies the nation behind the army he enlists. But Saul is deeply flawed. The king soon falls prey to darker spirits. He refuses to obey the divine restrictions placed on his rule. He wants to be a priest and prophet as well as a king. Saul is consumed by a spirit of jealousy.

Finally, the Lord rejects Saul and directs Samuel to anoint the youngest son of Jesse, the great-grandson of Ruth, as the chosen ruler. The reputation of young David, an unlikely warrior and court musician, grows in popularity. An enraged king attempts to assassinate David. David escapes with the help of Saul's son, Jonathon. The fugitive David gathers a gang of misfits who are forced to flee with their new leader into the wilderness and later across the border into enemy-controlled territory, with Saul's army in hot pursuit. Saul's heart grows darker with every passing day. After Saul dies in battle along with his son and heir Jonathon, David becomes king of Israel.

King David would rule the nation for forty years. Most of Israel's enemies would be subdued. Jerusalem, the great fortress city, would finally come under Israelite control and become the capitol of the nation. David, a warrior king with the heart of a musician, brings the Tabernacle and its Ark of the Covenant to Jerusalem. He longs to move the center of Hebrew worship from a tent to a permanent temple. He makes grand plans for a house worthy of the Lord. The Lord says, "No!" A man of peace, not a man with hands soiled by the blood of battle, must build the temple.

Later, David falls into temptation, commits adultery, and plots a murder to cover up his affair. One family problem after another scars what might have otherwise been the story of a great king. Near death, an elderly David pronounces his son Solomon, the next king.

King Solomon inherited a peaceful and prosperous nation. Wealth pours into his treasury through trade, tribute and taxes. The son realizes the dream of his father and builds a magnificent temple to the Lord God. The reputation of Solomon's wealth and wisdom spreads. Rulers far and wide come to Jerusalem to honor the famed king of Israel.

But as wise as Solomon may have been, he foolishly invited pagan wives and their "gods" into his palace. Soon, even the king's heart, despite all the good he had done, turns further and further from the heart of God. When Solomon dies, he leaves behind a personal legacy rich in wealth but poor in the real treasures of life. Rehoboam, Solomon's son and heir, proves ill-prepared for what awaits him as the next king of Israel. The stories of the Kingdom of Israel and its three great rulers are recorded in 1 Samuel 9-2 Samuel, and 1 Kings 1-11 and 1 Chronicles 10-2 Chronicles 9.

The Divided Kingdom. After a hundred years of greatness, the nation David and Solomon had worked so hard to build quickly disintegrates. Civil war breaks out when the new king refuses the advice of his elders to lower the burden of taxes. The nation splits in two. Ten of the twelve tribes followed rebel leader Jeroboam and declared their independence from Rehoboam and Jerusalem. The northern kingdom would retain the name Israel; the southern would be known as Judah.

In an effort to unify his rebel nation, Jeroboam built a rival temple to discourage his people from looking to Jerusalem as their center of faith. The faith of the northern kingdom soon degenerates into paganism and idolatry. Kings would come and go in both Judah and Israel. Coups and assassinations became common, especially in the North. Occasionally, the Lord would send prophets to call the wandering hearts of both nations back to faithfulness.

For a little less than two hundred years, the two sister nations would live side by side. Sometimes, they would confront one another in battle. At other times, the two would peacefully coexist. Both would take turns allying with and going to war against neighboring nations. After countless attempts to push back other aggressive enemies, Israel and its capital city of Samaria fell to the Assyrian Empire in 722 BC. Most of the people are taken captive and carried away to slavery in the conquering nation. Israel and its ten tribes would be no more. The Old Testament books of 1 Kings 12-2 Kings 16, as well as 2 Chronicles 10-28, record the events of the divided nation. Among the prophets who declared the word of the Lord during these troubled times were Amos, Jonah, Hosea, Isaiah, Micah, Obadiah, and Joel.

Judah Alone. The southern kingdom of Judah continued a precarious existence for another 136 years. Surrounding empires see it as easy prey. Through periods of decline and revival, the kings of Judah cling to power. The great temple of Solomon remains the center of Jewish worship and pride. Prophets, such as Jeremiah, Nahum, Habakkuk and Zephaniah, promise the protection of the Lord if the nation will only remain faithful to his covenant. Sometimes they are, but often they aren't.

The prophet Jeremiah warned the nation that its people would face seventy years of captivity if they continued to refuse to repent and turn wholeheartedly to God. Doubting the protection of their God, the kings of Judah seek the protection of larger nations or pay off would-be conquerors with tribute. Finally, all efforts to maintain their independence fail. These events are recorded in 2 Kings 17-25 and 2 Chronicles 29-36.

Exile in Babylon. Jerusalem fell to the Babylonians in 586 BC. First, the youngest and brightest are carried to Babylon, Daniel among them. Eventually, more and more of the citizenry were marched to the eastern nation as captives. In Babylon, the vanquished Jews mourn what was lost and yearn for a return. Without a temple and its priests, the Jewish religion developed new practices. Synagogues, with their rabbis and the study of the Torah, become the focus of the faith. True to the predictions of Jeremiah, the Jewish people remained in Babylon for seventy years. Jeremiah, Daniel, and Ezekiel sound the voice of the Lord to the exiles. The story is told in Daniel, Esther, and parts of Jeremiah.

The Return. Eventually, Persia conquered Babylon. Cyrus, the Persian ruler, releases the Jewish captives. The new king permits anyone who wants to return to their homeland. Some returned; some stayed. Other captives would make the long trek back to Jerusalem in the years to come. Zerubbabel leads the struggling returnees as they attempt to rebuild what was left of Jerusalem. Progress is slow. Ezra rallies the people to a deeper faith in God. Nehemiah, a trusted Jewish servant in the court of the Persian king, brings aid and encouragement to the desperate pilgrims.

Gradually, the walls of Jerusalem take shape and work on reconstructing the temple begins. The rebuilt city and the reimagined temple are a mere shadow of what they once were. The faithful cling to the promises of the prophets that one day, the Lord would send his Messiah, the anointed one as a new king like David, to once again return Israel to its golden days. The Old Testament library closes with a weak, struggling Jewish nation dreaming of a better future. The books of Ezra and Nehemiah contain the accounts of the struggling returnees. The prophets Haggai, Zechariah, and Malachi all seek to rally the people to greater faith.

Waiting for the Messiah. For nearly four hundred years, the Jewish people would await the promised Messiah. They would wait largely in silence. The prophets of old were few and far between. But still, the faithful waited and hoped. Independence would prove hard to keep. First, the Greeks and later the Romans would march from the West and lay claim to Judea. Heroic leaders, such as the Maccabees in the second century BC, would lead campaigns for freedom and restoration. But such moments of high hope seldom lasted long. By the dawn of a new era, the Jewish people had settled into a life of quiet serfdom under the boot of the mighty Roman Empire.

With the turn of the last page of the Old Testament library, a new story begins. The big *Story of Israel* awaits the Biggest Story. The old story had hinted at it. The prophets had pointed to it. Now it was here! An unlikely king from an unlikely place inaugurates a new kingdom. This time, it will not be the Kingdom of Israel. The new kingdom would be the Kingdom of God!

For a poetic summary of the *Story of Israel,* see Psalm 104, 105, and 106.

The New Testament contains brief summaries of the *Story of Israel* in three speeches found in the Acts of the Apostles: Acts 3:12-26, Acts 7:2-53, and Acts 13:16-41.

***

Going Deeper—Chapter 5

1. What is the big story of the Old Testament? Why is this important?

2. In what way is Genesis 1-11 a "preface" to the Old Testament story? What important information does it provide?

3. How does Genesis 12-50 provide the "backstory" for the rest of the Old Testament?

4. Review the list of the eight chapters of the *Story of Israel* until you can name them in order.

5. Read Psalms 104, 105, and 106. What's the significance of these songs?

6. Carefully read the three speeches in the Acts of the Apostles that review the *Story of Israel* (3:12-26; 7:2-53; 13:16-41). What part of the Old Testament story is emphasized in each? What was the point of these speeches?

Chapter 6: The Jesus Story

Are we there yet? We have all heard those words. A long family drive, perhaps to Grandma's for Thanksgiving or on the way to a long-awaited vacation, turns into a never-ending cry of impatience from the backseat, "Are we there yet?" "Just a little longer" only works for the first hundred miles. The questions gradually grow louder and more persistent. Are we there yet?

That's the question that brings us to the opening pages of the New Testament and the fourth chapter in the Story of God. For centuries, the Story of Israel had grown darker and darker. Corruption, invasion, exile, and captivity were followed by The Return. Back home, the Jewish people found their homeland and its temple in shambles. The hard work of rebuilding began. The result only reminded the people of the glory that once was and would never be again.

But the prophets had promised a brighter future. They had said the glory of Israel would one day be restored. But when? For four-hundred years after The Return, Israel waited. The longer they waited, the more impatient they became. A few bright moments only managed to build and then dash their hopes anew. Foreign invaders once again overran Israel—this time Alexander the Great and the Greek hordes. For a few heroic moments, the Jews fought back. Soon, the Roman legions took up where the Greeks had left off. Were the prophets wrong?

When we finally turn the page after the long slog through the thirty-nine books of the Old Testament, we are finally there! As the New Testament opens, we enter a new chapter in the Story of God. But this next chapter holds more than a few surprises. The New Testament continues the story that began in the Old Testament but with a totally unexpected twist. The Old Testament told the story of how God had called a man (Abram) and the chosen nation (Israel) that resulted. Few would have guessed that in this next chapter, God doesn't call a man. God becomes a man.

The New Testament is the Story of Jesus and the community of faith that resulted. The Old Testament may have been the Big Story, but the New Testament contains the Biggest Story. The New Testament tells how the Word of God, the Creator of all, became a man and dwelt among us (Jn 1:1-14). He walked the earth. People watched him perform miracles in the power of God and listened to him teach the mysteries of God with the authority of heaven. Few expected the Story of Jesus. Certainly, no one anticipated what would happen thirty-three years later.

To fully appreciate the magnitude of the Story of Jesus, we must overcome one major temptation. Because of the sheer size of the Old Testament (75% of the Bible), we can be lulled into ignoring the preeminence of the New Testament and how it differs from the Old. The New is more than a continuation of the Old. The two are related. But the two are not equal. The Old provides information needed to understand the New. It leads to the New. But the Old must never be allowed to overshadow the New. In the New Testament, something totally different and unique thrusts itself on the pages of the Bible. The Story of Jesus towers over the Story of Israel.

The fallacy of the "level Bible" presents a persistent problem for Bible readers. As a result, some endeavor to follow Old Testament laws and rituals as if they were a necessary part of the gospel. Others counter the teachings of Jesus about love for one's neighbor and forgiveness with appeals to Old Testament calls for vengeance and militant justice. A few through the ages have tried to tack Old Testament customs on to the gospel, thinking that such practices demonstrate a deeper brand of faith. In truth, anything added to Jesus always results in a lesser, not a greater, faith. The Old Testament matters. But it must always be read as the introduction to the New Testament, never its equal.

The New Testament Library

When we open the New Testament, we are once again confronted with a library of books. This time, the library contains twenty-seven separate volumes. The combination to this New Testament library is 4-1-21-1. We label the first four—gospels a type of biography of Jesus. We will discuss this more in a moment. The fifth book (Acts of the Apostles) falls into the history category—the story of the first Christians. The next twenty-one are all letters or, using the more formal term—epistles. These letters come in a variety of forms. Some are very personal; others are more like essays. At least thirteen come from the pen of the Apostle Paul, sometimes through assistants who wrote as he dictated.

A variety of authors wrote the remaining eight. The last book in the library falls under the heading of prophecy. Many readers find Revelation troublesome, even scary. In reality, it contains a message of hope. The book paints a dramatic picture of the future faced by followers of Jesus and the climactic end that the Lord has in store for history. Revelation provides a fitting conclusion to the Story of God.

The Fourfold Gospel

As we open the New Testament, we first need to understand the word "gospel." The English term translates the Greek word from which we get "evangel" or "evangelism." Literally, it means "good news." Originally, this "good news" might often refer to the announcement of a king's planned visit to a city. Heralds would precede the arrival with the announcement so the citizens could give the monarch an appropriate reception.

In a sense, to apply this word to Jesus was something close to a political statement. The gospels declared that the true Lord of lords and King of kings had arrived. All who heard the announcement were called to give him the allegiance that belonged to no other. Clearly, the Jewish leaders, and especially Pilate, understood the implications of Jesus's claims (Jn 18:33-40).

In reality, these four gospels are not pure biographies in the sense of neutral observations. They are declarations that a new king has arrived on the scene and everyone should acknowledge his authority. But this does not mean that they aren't presenting an accurate account of his life and teachings. They are history, but history with a purpose.

The four gospels are similar but not identical. The main message comes through loud and clear. But each presents a decidedly different perspective on the life of Jesus. This should not be surprising, much less troubling. Have any four people observe the same series of events. Ask them later to describe what they saw. Each may tell a slightly different story. One may concentrate on one set of facts, another on different details. Both can be accurate but viewed from a different perspective. So, it is with the four accounts of Jesus's life.

The first three are quite similar; the last is quite different. For that reason, Matthew, Mark, and Luke are often called the "Synoptics" from a term meaning "same view." Many scholars believe that Mark may have been written first. Matthew and Luke came later, both following Mark's outline while adding bits and pieces of information not included in Mark. In fact, Matthew, probably the most literate of Jesus's twelve disciples as a tax collector, could have kept notes during Jesus's ministry, some of which Mark may have used to compose his first account. Luke, a highly educated Greek physician, claims to have researched the story and included significant information not found in Matthew or Mark (Lk 1:1-4). Matthew and Mark may have known very little about the birth and early life of Jesus. Luke included these stories, possibly after interviewing Mary and others who knew Jesus before he began his public ministry and called his first disciples.

Different Gospels for Different Folks

The four books also differ due to the different audiences to which they were written. Matthew is the most Jewish of the four. He begins with a genealogy that goes back to Abraham, the beginning of the family tree of Israel. He also demonstrates a great interest in the Messiah's fulfillment of Old Testament prophesy. Mark, on the other hand, seems aimed at a non-Jewish audience. When he references Jewish customs or terms, he explains their meaning. Also, his account is action-packed and fast-moving. His use of the word "immediately" stands out. The traditions from the second and third centuries claim that Mark became an associate of Peter's, eventually traveling to Rome. Thus, he writes for the benefit of non-Jewish believers in the Roman church. Luke writes with a broad brush. His genealogy traces Jesus's ancestry all the way to Adam. He especially seems interested in Jesus's contact with Gentiles, as well as women, the poor, and the outcast. He may have had a Greek cosmopolitan reader in mind.

John, on the other hand, reads very differently from the other three. The assumption is that the fourth gospel was written last, probably thirty years or so after the others. John may have wanted to fill in the blanks left by the first three. He highlights Jesus's ministry in Judea, while the other three spend the majority of their time on his work in Galilee. John also seems very aware of the challenges facing the church at the end of the first century. His opening introduction, in particular, targets some of the issues created by the gospel's confrontation with outside philosophies. The combination of Greek dualism and popular mystery religions, known to history as gnosticism, would develop into a serious problem in years to come. John's gospel, as does his later letters, anticipates and seeks to inoculate the church to this eventuality.

For Matthew, Jesus is the Jewish messiah who fulfills the Old Testament. Mark presents Jesus as the mighty Son of God who demonstrates all the power and authority of the King of kings and Lord of lords. Luke introduces the Son of Man, who is the savior of the world, including the least, the last, and the lost. John proclaims the Word of God, who reveals and makes known the Father.

Four Gospels: One Story

A Bible reader must never lose sight of the fact that the Christian gospel is the Story of Jesus. He is the focus of the faith. Any genuine witness to the faith always points to Jesus. "We proclaim Him" (Col 1:28). This can easily get lost in the traditions, activities, and competing interests of those who follow him. The gospel is about Jesus, not the church! It is not primarily about the sacraments, rituals, and practices that occupy his people. Jesus is the focus of the gospel, not the men and women who often stand in the spotlight. It is about Jesus, not about ethics and morality. It is certainly not about politics, current or ancient. The gospel is also not about justice and liberty for the poor and oppressed unless that effort also includes a strong emphasis on Jesus's atoning, death and resurrection. To understand the gospel, we must major in reading and learning about the life and ministry of Jesus.

So, what is the Story of Jesus? The four gospels focus on eight facets of Jesus' life. Together, these eight provide a full, multi-dimensional portrait of Christ. Any accurate witness to Jesus will include these facts.

His Prophetic Birth

The Jewish faithful had long anticipated the coming of the Messiah by the end of the first century BC. They had suffered long enough, they thought, under the tyranny of first the Greeks and then the Romans. Their prophets had long promised a deliverer who would usher in the Kingdom of God. Many expected something political. Jesus would prove to be someone far more revolutionary!

Matthew, in particular, emphasizes the prophecies fulfilled at Jesus's birth. He wanted his fellow Jews to know that Jesus was the real deal. A forerunner would come first, then a king would be born of a virgin in the only fitting place—Bethlehem, the home of King David. But it would not all be laughter and joy. After the visit of strangers from the East, Herod would unleash his fury against an imagined rival. Babies would die; mothers would suffer in grief. Egypt would play a role in the birth of the King, just as it had in the birth of the nation. Eventually, Jesus would find his way to Nazareth, the label "Nazarene," perhaps fulfilling the promise that a branch would grow out of the severed stump of Jesse. The Greek word Nazarene sounds like the Hebrew word for "branch," referred to in the promises of the coming king.

Mark skips the birth of Jesus, jumping right to John the Baptist, who prepares for the ministry of the Messiah. Luke, on the other hand, researches what Matthew may have known little about (Lk 1:1-4). He writes of John the Baptist's parents, Jesus's mother, Mary, and numerous other characters who populate the story of Jesus's birth. These include the shepherds, angels, and faithful servants waiting in the temple for their King (Lk 2). John mentions the coming of Jesus in the most profound and philosophical manner. This was more than just the birth of another prophet, John insists. In Jesus, we witness the self-revelation of the Creator himself. "The Word became flesh" (Jn 1:14)!

His Exemplary Life

Jesus grew to manhood. When the time was right, he was baptized of John "to fulfill all righteousness" (Mt 3:15). He then marched straight into the jaws of temptation. He faced the same moral struggles every man and woman faced. Yet he was without sin (Heb 4:15). Throughout his life, he practiced what he preached. He taught love, and he loved the outcast and the sinner. He said to turn the other cheek and he did in response to the most vicious attacks. He taught his disciples to pray and he prayed. He was faithful to his calling and to his heavenly Father in every way.

For that reason, those who followed Him could call all believers "to walk as Jesus walked." (1 Jn 2:6). They were taught to live holy lives just as they learned from Christ (Eph 4:20). The apostles exhorted Christians to walk "in His steps" as they faced adversity and persecution (1 Pt 2:21). Jesus alone could be our intercessor because he too faced temptation yet without sin (Heb 2:18). The Christian's standard of conduct is never the norms of society, the traditions of those who have gone before them, much less the lifestyles of the rich and famous. Jesus alone is the example.

His Amazing Miracles

Jesus demonstrated the power of God through miracles and healing. In Mark, his works of wonder appear at the turn of almost every page. He heals the sick, raises the dead, cleanses lepers, casts out demons, feeds multitudes, and calms the storms. John, in particular, emphasizes seven miracles, which he calls "signs." These particular miracles point to something noteworthy about the person and power of Christ. Jesus turns water into wine that proved better than the best that man could offer (2:1-11). He heals a nobleman's son while miles way (4:46-54). Distance proves no barrier to him. He restores a man's legs left useless for thirty-eight years (5:1-15). Jesus healed the scars of time. He feeds a multitude with mere scraps of food (6:5-14). In the wine, he was the Lord of quality; in the bread, he became the Lord of quantity. He alone is the bread of life that truly satisfies. Even the norms of creation must yield to the Creator when Jesus walks on water (6:16-21). He brings sight to a man born blind (9:1-7). He can reverse the worst of life's misfortunes. Last but certainly not least, Jesus brings Lazarus to life after four days in the grave (11:1-45). Even death, the last enemy, proved no match for the Author of Life.

His Challenging Teachings

Everyone recognized Jesus as a teacher. They called him rabbi for a good reason. Disciples and adversaries alike were amazed at his words.

He didn't teach to curry men's favor. The traditions of the past never proved a boundary for his lessons. His teachings sometimes confused his disciples, annoyed the authorities, angered his rivals, and delighted the multitudes. But Jesus's teachings often concealed sharp barbs that could hook the unsuspecting hearer.

The Sermon on the Mount exemplifies Jesus's most powerful lessons. He turned the normal priorities of society on their head. He outlined an "upside down kingdom." He defied the simplifications of the Law of Moses. He made morality deeper and broader than many had dared to imagine. He exposed the root of sin. He called for priorities beyond wealth and status.

Jesus's parables also illustrated his teachings in profound and sometimes confusing ways. Only the most serious would listen deeply enough to hear the truth embedded in the story. He taught love, forgiveness, servanthood, and readiness for heaven's future invasion of Planet Earth. Most of all, he taught with unmatched authority.

His Atoning Death

The highpoint of Jesus's life was his death. Many thought it was proof of his failure. Little did they know! He had insisted over and over again, much to the dismay of his disciples, that he came to lay down his life as a ransom. He told them, "he must go to Jerusalem and suffer many things at the hands of the elders, the chief priests, and the teachers of the law, and that he must be killed and on the third day be raised to life" (Mt 16:21-22).

The events surrounding his death were so vital to his mission that the four gospels spent more time detailing the day-by-day events of his final week than any other time in his life. Matthew devotes a fourth of his account to Jesus's final days; Mark almost a third; Luke a fifth; and John almost half. All the events of Jesus's life matter, but none more than what happened on Good Friday and Easter Sunday. The "word of the cross" becomes the message of the church (1 Cor 1:18). But what happened three days after the cross would change everything.

His Victorious Resurrection

Jesus died on the cross. He was buried in a borrowed tomb. Many may have thought that was the end of the story. It wasn't! On the third day, he arose just as he predicted. The resurrection of Jesus from the dead provided the exclamation point at the end of a marvelous life. The resurrection vindicated his claims and authority. As Paul would later insist, he was "appointed the Son of God in power by his resurrection from the dead: Jesus Christ our Lord" (Rm 1:4).

While no human actually witnessed the moment of the resurrection itself, eye witnesses testified that the tomb was empty despite the best attempts of the powers that be to keep it sealed and free from tampering. Angels announced the news to skeptical disciples, "He is not here. He has risen from the dead." Later, Jesus himself appeared, first to the women who had come to complete the burial process and later to those who doubted their report. He met with his followers and even invited them to inspect the wounds from his crucifixion. He talked with them, ate with them, and carefully taught them that his victory over the grave provided further evidence that he was who he claimed to be. He showed them how the entire Old Testament had pointed to this moment. His entire life, ministry, death, and resurrection fulfilled all that the Story of Israel had promised.

Without the resurrection, the gospel would not be good news. It would merely be the story of another martyr who died at the hands of ruthless authorities. The cross would forever be the symbol of hate, not an expression of divine love and grace. Jesus's claims to be the Son of God and the path to eternal life would sound like the foolish rantings of a mad man. His teachings would lose their appeal. Who would want to follow a man so misguided and confused?

The resurrection changes everything. The last enemy has been conquered. The door to eternal life has been opened. "Death is swallowed up in victory" (1 Cor 15:54). The fear of death is gone (Heb 2:15). The crucifixion was not the end of the Jesus Story. It was but a brief pause. Three days later, the story came roaring back. The victorious resurrection marked the beginning of a new chapter in the Story of God.

His Glorious Ascension and Heavenly Ministry

Forty days after the resurrection, Jesus gathered his disciples, delivered his parting instructions, and ascended to heaven (Acts 1:1-11). Mission accomplished! But a new mission was beginning. He had told them it was to their advantage that he go away. He would not leave them alone. They would not become spiritual orphans. He promised to send another helper, the Holy Spirit (Jn 14:15-19; 16:7). This third person of the Godhead would bring the power of heaven into their lives. The Spirit's invisible yet very personal presence would launch them into a whole new dimension of ministry.

The task of spreading his message would forever be a co-mission. Jesus would continue to work with his ambassadors (Mt 28:18-20). The power of the Holy Spirit would work with them and in them. That became a reality on Pentecost (Acts 2:1-4). Jesus had kept his promise. Months before, he had said, "Let anyone who is thirsty come to me and drink. Whoever believes in me, as Scripture has said, rivers of living water will flow from within them." John would add a word of explanation, "By this, he meant the Spirit, whom those who believed in him were later to receive. Up to that time, the Spirit had not been given since Jesus had not yet been glorified" (Jn 7:37-39). Jesus ascended, was glorified, and his ministry now continued through a Spirit-empowered church.

Scripture also points to another facet of Jesus' continuing ministry. The writer of Hebrews insists that in his ongoing priestly ministry, "he always lives to intercede for them" (Heb 7:25). Paul makes the same point when he writes, "Christ Jesus who died—more than that, who was raised to life—is at the right hand of God and is also interceding for us" (Rm 8:34). His followers are not alone. He works with them as they spread his message (Mt 28:20).

His Promised Return

Jesus taught his disciples that his death, resurrection, and ascension to glory were not the end. He would return. He came the first time in lowliness and humiliation. He came as the Suffering Servant (Isa 53:1-12). When he comes again, he said, it would be in power and glory (Mt 24:30-31). He promised his disciples, "I am going there to prepare a place for you? And if I go and prepare a place for you, I will come back and take you to be with me that you also may be where I am" (Jn 14:2-3). The closer his departure came, the more Jesus worked to prepare his disciples for what would soon happen.

He warned that they would face tough days before his eventual return. They would face persecution from the outside and false teachers from the inside. Evil and sin would grow worse and worse.

They needed to be ready for what was to come. He also told them in no uncertain terms that trying to predict his return was futile. "But about that day or hour, no one knows, not even the angels in heaven, nor the Son, but only the Father... So you also must be ready because the Son of Man will come at an hour when you do not expect him." (Mt 24:36, 44). The challenge for them was to be ready for the long haul yet to expect his return at any time.

His return will mean judgment and wrath for the unbeliever but hope, life, and reward for those who look forward to that day. Jesus said, "Very truly I tell you, whoever hears my word and believes him who sent me has eternal life and will not be judged but has crossed over from death to life. Very truly, I tell you, a time is coming and has now come when the dead will hear the voice of the Son of God and those who hear will live" (Jn 5:24-25).

Jesus's teachings about his return mirror the last chapter in the Story of God, the Coronation. On that day, he will be acknowledged as King of kings and Lord of lords. Every knee will bow and every tongue will confess that he is Lord (Phil 2:10-11). Meanwhile, followers of Jesus live in the "in-between-times." His kingdom is both "now and not yet." Believers live in a world enslaved to sin and evil, but they order their lives in anticipation of his glorious return. We are the ones "on whom the culmination of the ages has come" (1 Cor 10:11). He is coming again. What a day that will be!

***

The Story of Jesus is the Biggest Story, unimaginable Good News. The Old Testament pointed forward to his coming. Jesus fulfilled the promises of the Old Testament and announced the invasion of the Kingdom of God. A new king had come. A new day had dawned. The Story isn't over. But because of Jesus, we know how it ends!

***

Going Deeper—Chapter 6

1. How does the story of the Old Testament differ from the Good News of the New Testament?

2. What is the "fallacy of the level Bible?" Why does this matter?

3. How do the four Gospels differ? Which is your "favorite" and why?

4. Name the eight facets of Jesus's life outlined in the Gospels. Provide a two or three-sentence summary of each.

5. Which of Jesus's teachings do you find the most challenging? Why?

Chapter 7: The Story of the First Christians

The eight-year-old boy raced into the kitchen after school. His mother waited with his afternoon snack as usual. But instead of heading for the food, the boy immediately ran to his mother and breathlessly asked, "Mom, where did I come from?"

"Oh, no!" mom thought to herself, "It's time for 'The Talk.' I'm not ready for this!" Mom took a deep breathe, sat her son down on a stool, and began the dreaded explanation. The youngster listened intently while munching on his PB&J. His mom went into great detail explaining the "birds and the bees."

When finished, she asked him if he had any questions. The boy looked at her with a curious look on his face and said, "That's interesting, Mom, but we had a new boy in class today. He told me he came from Cleveland. So I just wanted to know where I came from."

Where we come from can prove interesting on several levels. Most of us become curious about our origins from time to time. We listen to the stories of our grandparents and older uncles and aunts. We trace our family tree. We look at old pictures. We want to know where we came from. We instinctively know that where we come from tells a lot about who we are.

As we turn another page in the Story of God, we come to an important "origin story." This first section of the chapter on the Co-mission explains the beginnings of the church. When we look at the churches in our communities, we know they didn't just pop up out of nowhere like mushrooms. They came from somewhere. The same is true of the church-at-large. The church had a beginning.

Much more history will follow in the next two-thousand years, but those all-important beginning years will help explain the fruit that grows from those roots. That beginning will tell us much about the nature of the church and possibly its purpose. We may learn why churches do what they do. In some cases, as we read this part of the Bible, we may find ourselves asking, "Why don't we do what those first Christians did? Why aren't we more like them?"

The fifth book of the New Testament, known to us as the Acts of the Apostles, forms a bridge between Christ and the church. Jesus claimed to be the Messiah, the Son of God. He explained that his death was part of God's eternal plan for saving lost men and women from the power of sin and death. He insisted that every chapter in the Story of God that had preceded his coming was in preparation for his arrival. All that came before pointed to him. After he completed his task, he gave his followers the task of spreading that message around the world. But, and this is important, he insisted that they were not alone in that mission. He would continue to be with them. Through the Holy Spirit, he would guide and empower them. They were not alone. Theirs, indeed, was a co-mission.

Luke's Story: Volume Two

The author of Acts is clearly the same writer who penned the third gospel. He addresses both to someone he identifies as Theophilus. The Greek word means "friend of God." The term could be a proper name, or perhaps a nickname, or even a title. In any case, Luke addresses him with the same term in both books. In the opening lines of Acts, he notes that this is a followup to a previous volume about the life and ministry of Jesus (Acts 1:1-2). He had written previously about what Jesus began to do and teach. He now tells the rest of the story!

Identifying exactly who the author is requires a bit of detective work. Later in Acts (16:10), the writer begins to describe the travels of Paul in the first person plural (we). At other times, he writes in the third person (he or they). Clearly, the writer was a companion of Paul and company part of the time. At other times, he wasn't. A careful comparison of Paul's travels and his letters, where he often mentions those who are with him, leads to the conclusion that the most likely person to have been with Paul at the appropriate times was Luke, and therefore the author of this account. That, then, provides the reason for attributing the third gospel to Luke.

In his letter to the Colossians (4:14), Paul refers to Luke as "the beloved physician." Most likely, Luke was a Greek convert who may have joined Paul in Troas on his second missionary journey. Luke was an eyewitness to many of the later events he wrote about. The remaining information he could have gathered in much the same way as he did with his account of Jesus's life and ministry. He investigated, researched, and likely conducted personal interviews where possible (Lk 1:1-4).

A reader might rightly consider the traditional title a bit misleading. The book might more appropriately be called "some of the acts of some of the apostles." In this case, the list of main characters includes primarily Peter and Paul, with a few other men and women thrown in as supporting actors. Peter appears as the central figure in chapters one through twelve, with Paul taking over in the remainder of the book.

They Were First Called Christians

Acts tell the story of the first Christians. Their DNA runs through the veins of every follower of Jesus since that day. Ironically, no one used the term Christian for the first fifteen years. At the beginning, they were simply known as disciples. During Jesus's ministry, men and women from all walks of life traveled with him, some for short periods of time. Others were with him from beginning to end. He was the teacher. They were the students or disciples. Early in Acts, that identity continued. The connection with Jesus was the most important part. They taught what He had taught them. They endeavored to mold their lives according to their master's example. The message they proclaimed pointed back to Jesus. They always focused the spotlight on him, never themselves. Even their adversaries recognized their connection with Jesus (Acts 4:13).

Somewhere along the line, another name became associated with these disciples of Jesus. When Saul (later Paul) sought official documents to pursue and arrest these Jesus followers, he referred to them as people who "belonged to the Way" (Acts 9:2). Later, Paul himself would encounter skeptics who "became obstinate; they refused to believe and publicly maligned the Way" (Acts 19:9). A riot ensued that Luke described as a "disturbance about the Way" (Acts 19:23). In one of his first hearings after his arrest, Paul acknowledges that he was a Jew who worshipped the God of his ancestors "as a follower of the Way" (Acts 24:14). Even Felix, the Roman governor, was acquainted with the Way (Acts 24:22). Likely, the term derived from Jesus' teaching about the "narrow way that leads to life" (Matt 7:14) and his claim that "I am the way and the truth and the life. No one comes to the Father except through me" (Jn 14:6). Both adversaries and adherents recognized that these first Christians remained devoted to Jesus.

Eventually, a new label developed. Luke simply notes that "they were called Christians first at Antioch" (Acts 11:26). He leaves unclear whether the believers themselves adopted the term or if critics coined it as a derogatory slur. Whatever the source, the name stuck. Two thousand years later, it remains the most common term for those who claim Jesus as Lord and Savior.

Even if no one knows the source of the name, it may be significant that it first occurred at Antioch. Totally apart from their apostolic leaders in Jerusalem, an unnamed band of Jesus' followers crossed a line that no one had dared cross before. They intentionally began to share the message of Jesus with non-Jews (Acts 11:20-21). This church that resulted would become the sending church for Paul and the missionary endeavors that would follow. The rest is history!

From Jerusalem to the World

The outline of Acts follows the directive Jesus gave his apostles at his parting. "You will be my witnesses in Jerusalem, and in all Judea and Samaria, and to the ends of the earth" (Acts 1:8). The first few chapters of Acts record the early years of the faith in Jerusalem and the surrounding region of Judea (Acts 1:1-6:7). Eventually, the gospel spread to the despised Samaritans (Acts 6:8-9:31). The gospel took the first turn toward the "ends of the earth" with the conversion of the Roman centurion Cornelius, a Gentile. Cornelius, a God-fearer who respected and supported the Jews, had never taken the big step of conversion. In a sense, Cornelius stood halfway between Jew and Gentile. Paul's conversion on the Damascus Road and eventual commission as a missionary sent out from the Antioch church would push the gospel into whole new frontiers. From that point on, the world became the mission field.

The First Christian's Top Ten

If a modern television producer set out to document the top ten events in Luke's record of the first Christians, she might have a hard time limiting the list to ten. In Acts, history is being made at the turn of almost every page. But certainly, such a list would include:

1. The Ascension of Jesus—Acts 1:9-11. That's where Acts begins. In this way, Luke links this volume with his previous work. This is not a new story; it is the second chapter of the Story of Jesus. Jesus had promised to be with his disciples in their future mission. He promises the power and resources that they would need. He will not leave them adrift in the brave new world they will face. Whatever happens in the story of these first Christians, Jesus remains at the center of everything.

2. The Replacement of Judas—Acts 1:12-26. This may not seem all that important to us, but clearly, it was to the first disciples. Because the story was ultimately about Jesus, it remained important that the circle be closed. Jesus called twelve apostles as witnesses to his ministry and committed them to a special task. So twelve it must be!

In the restricted sense here, an apostle was one of the twelve specifically chosen by Jesus to spread his teachings (Lk 6:13-16). With Judas out of the picture, Peter and the disciples who gathered in the Upper Room considered it important to fill the traitor's open position. The requirements were that this person have been with Jesus from his baptism by John until the ascension (Acts 1:21-22).

They prayed, cast lots, and selected Matthias as the twelfth apostle. Twelve may have been an important number because they saw themselves in a parallel role to the twelve sons of Jacob, the founding fathers of Israel. The testimony of these eyewitnesses about what Jesus did and taught would become the foundation of these first Christians' faith (Acts 2:42). Later, Saul-turned-Paul would join the band of apostles through the special intervention of Jesus himself.

3. Pentecost and the Rapid Spread of the Faith—Acts 2-6. One hundred twenty prayed and waited just as Jesus had instructed them. Then it happened! Jesus kept his promise. The predictions of the Old Testament prophets came true. Jesus was glorified. The Spirit was poured out. The church was born. That huddled mass of anxious disciples was transformed into a Spirited-powered, gospel-preaching, world-changing church on the march. Peter explained the message about Jesus. Thousand responded. A community of faith was born. These new disciples didn't just believe the gospel. They lived it. They shared it. The message spread. Opponents took notice. Soon, the fledgling church confronted rough waters.

4. The Martyrdom of Stephen—Acts 7. A promising young Greek-speaking disciple named Stephen drew the attention of the wrong people. Jewish scholars and their leaders argued with Stephen about the claims of Jesus to no avail. Their frustration quickly turned to anger and ultimately to violence. They charged him with blasphemy against the Lord, his temple, the Law, and, perhaps more importantly, their traditions. Nothing short of death would do. An execution crowd quickly assembled.

The leaders allow Stephen to speak. He preaches the longest and perhaps one of the most powerful messages in the entire book of Acts. He retells the Story of Israel, ending with the charge that this generation had killed God's Righteous One just like their forefathers had killed the prophets. That was the straw that broke the proverbial camel's back. The stones flew fast and furious. Stephen died a martyr at peace with his God and confident in his future. Luke footnotes the account of Stephen's death with the first introduction of Saul (Paul). He is pictured as a young onlooker who guards the coats of the executioners as they finish their grisly task.

5. The Conversion of Saul—Acts 9:1-31. No one would have expected what would soon become of that young bystander. Saul soon rises in the ranks of the Jerusalem religious community. He zealously pursued others whom he thought deserved the same fate as Stephen. Learning of a stronghold of disciples in far-off Damascus, he secures the proper documents to bring these fugitives across the border and back to Judea. Saul is serious and single-minded. Little does he know what is about to happen.

On his way to Damascus, the risen and glorified Jesus confronts the persecutor-in-chief. Saul is blinded by a light. He will learn he has met the Light of the World! Days later, Saul arrives in Damascus, a changed man. He becomes one of those he had pursued. Ananias baptizes the new convert. As passionate as always, Saul boldly shares his new found faith. Few know what to make of him.

Eventually, he escapes Damascus and retraces his steps back to Jerusalem. Once in Jerusalem, only Barnabas trusts him enough to intercede and introduce Saul to the church leaders. Eventually, the Jerusalem Christians send him home to Tarsus for his own safety. As far as they know, Saul is out of the picture for good. God knew differently.

6. Cornelius and the Gospel to the Gentiles (Acts 10:1-11:18). Saul (Paul) will eventually become the primary missionary to non-

Jews. But before that endeavor could ever be taken seriously by the fledgling Christian community, someone else would have to open the door. Only one man had the standing and influence to cross that line first—Peter. Like Saul on the Damascus Road, the Lord confronts Peter on a rooftop in Joppa. The Lord had closed the eyes of Saul the persecutor. The Lord opens the eyes of Peter, the preacher.

Reluctantly, Peter accepts the fact that many of the restrictions of the old covenant no longer apply. This meant that as a follower of Jesus, Peter needed to open his life to new foods and, more importantly, new people. No sooner had Peter accepted this notion in theory than he received a knock on his door. He is directed to the home of Cornelius, a Gentile who was ready and willing to hear about Jesus. Cornelius accepts Christ on the same terms as the Jewish believers before him. The door was open.

7. The Sending of the First Missionaries—(Acts 11:19-30; 12:25; 13:1-3). As noted previously, the disciples were first called Christians in Antioch. The Lord used this church, not the church in Jerusalem, to launch an entirely new venture. No doubt, missionaries had spread the gospel before. But none had set their sights on non-Jews. The church at Antioch had begun with a different vision. The Antioch church saw their non-Jewish neighbors as potential brothers and sisters in the faith. Not content to preach the gospel at home, they looked beyond their own borders.

The leaders of the church recruited Barnabas and Saul as their representatives. The two were first sent with a relief offering for the famine-stricken believers in Judea. No sooner had the two returned than their church sent them out again, this time as missionaries. The two would cross oceans and mountains with the message of Jesus.

Most significantly, they crossed ethnic and cultural barriers with the Good News. And people responded!

8. The Jerusalem Council and the Big Decision—Acts 15:1-35. The domestic and foreign outreach of the church at Antioch drew the attention of the Jerusalem church. Some from Jerusalem weren't so sure about this new direction. More Jewish-oriented preachers from Judea insisted that the Antioch approach and the work of Saul and Barnabas needed some refinement. Gentiles could become Christians, they agreed, but only after they first converted to Judaism. They taught that to come to Christ, a person had to first come through Moses. This had never been a problem as long as all the new Christians came from the ranks of the Jews. But, the success of the Antioch church and its missionaries had changed everything. Somebody needed to solve this new dilemma.

Saul and Barnabas were sent to Jerusalem to confer with the senior Christian leaders. Their goal—to reach a consensus about how to bring non-Jews into the fellowship of faith. No one can overestimate how significant this meeting was for the future of the church. This was a watershed moment.

The leaders met. They prayed. They talked, debated, and listened to one another. Most of all, they endeavored to listen to the will of God. Their conclusion—anyone could become a follower of Jesus by simply believing and obeying the gospel. Gentiles need not become Jews. The law of Moses was in the past. Jewish believers could continue their traditions and culture as long as they didn't confuse those practices with the gospel. Gentiles were not required to adopt Jewish culture and traditions, but they should respect it. Gentile believers should try not to antagonize and disrespect their Jewish brothers and sisters by flaunting the Gentile practices that were so abhorrent to Jewish traditions.

The leaders composed a letter to that effect and sent copies to churches far and wide. A new day of outreach and fellowship had dawned. The church was on its way to becoming a global enterprise.

9. Paul's Missionary Journeys—Acts 13:1-14:29; 15:36-20:38. No one would play a larger role in the spread of the Christian message than Saul, eventually known as Paul. The main persecutor had become the main missionary. Paul and Barnabas carried the gospel to Cyprus and then to Asia Minor (what is known on today's maps as western Turkey). Later, the two would part company and go their separate ways. Paul and his new partner Silas once again visit the churches previously established in Galatia and surrounding territories. Prevented from going further east, they venture west into Macedonia and Greece. Everywhere they go, they confront both opportunities and opposition. But the news of Christ moves forward. The church of Jesus Christ establishes beachheads in scores of previously untouched places.

10. Paul's Arrest and Pending Trial in Rome—Acts 21-28. Paul dreams of going farther west, maybe as far as Spain. First, he must complete an unfinished task. He had been encouraging the Gentile churches that he established to never forget their brothers and sisters in Judea, where it had all started. Paul encouraged them to contribute money to help the Jewish believers who were facing ongoing famine and hardship. Paul gathered the monies with the intent of hand delivering it to the elders in Jerusalem. He wanted to personally assure them of the love and concern of the Gentile churches.

The goodwill trip turned into what some might have considered a disaster. In reality, the Lord was opening a different door for Paul and the gospel. A misunderstanding in the Jewish temple turns into a confrontation. A riot ensues. Roman security guards take Paul into protective custody. Jewish authorities brought charges of blasphemy and sedition against him. Events spiral out of control. To thwart an assassination attempt, the Roman officials transferred Paul to Caesarea and a more secure military facility for his own protection.

Caught up in government bureaucracy and corruption, Paul appeals his case to Caesar. The locals have no choice but to ship Paul to Rome. Eventually, after months of misadventures, Paul arrives in Rome. He remains a prisoner, confined to house arrest until his case weaves its way through the Roman legal system. Acts ends with Paul imprisoned but continuing to tell the Story of Jesus to any who come his way. Luke's last words were chosen with care. Paul was under arrest, but the gospel wasn't!

The Legacy of the First Christians

Luke ends Acts abruptly with Paul still in Roman custody. Luke never reports the outcome of Paul's trial. He offers no explanation. He simply ends the story. Perhaps Luke intends Theophilus and future readers of his account to realize that the story is not over. New chapters are being written every day wherever believers in Christ live and share the gospel. Our churches continue to live in the legacy of those first Christians.

What was that legacy? Four lessons stand out:

These first Christians proclaimed the Jesus Story. Wherever they went, they never forgot Jesus. Jesus, not their traditions, their culture or their politics, was the hope of the world. They told friends and strangers alike that Jesus was the savior of all who would come to him. Jesus lived, died on the cross, and arose from the grave so that sinners might have a fresh start with the Living God. This same Jesus was coming again to judge the living and the dead. Everyone must decide what to do with the truth about Jesus.

The first Christians faced opposition at every turn. Jesus had said they would. Sometimes, it was outright persecution. Martyrs gave their lives for their faith. At other times, the believers lived with low-grade hostility and indifference. But they didn't give up. They stood their ground and continued to point any who would listen to Jesus. They wanted everyone to know that Jesus was the reason for the way they lived and the way they would die if necessary.

These early believers also stood united. They cared for one another, supported one another, and lived life together. Unity mattered because a divided church could never represent the Prince of Peace, who promised to bring people together. But unity didn't come easy. As the faith spread, they faced new challenges. Language differences, cultural differences, and racial divides forced the church to confront and overcome their differences. They learned that differences didn't have to divide them. Those differences could make them stronger as long as their faith stayed focused on Jesus.

The young church quickly learned to cross barriers. Geographic boundaries fell first. Jesus had pointed them in that direction when he told them to move from Jerusalem onto Judea, then to Samaria and ultimately beyond. Staying the same and remaining in the same place was not an option. From its earliest days, the church was a missionary church. Some with limited vision may have wanted to keep the faith closer to home. But others knew that would never do. It was not "our church" first versus missionary work. It was Jesus first.

As long as the message of Jesus remained the focus, the church could never let borders become barriers. Obviously, crossing geographical boundaries meant confronting racial and ethnic divides. These can prove much harder to cross. But they must be crossed because in Christ "there is neither Jew nor Gentile, neither slave nor free, nor is there male and female, for you are all one in Christ Jesus" (Gal 3:28). These first Christians believed that claim.

***

Acts tell the story of the continuing work of Jesus through his people, the church. It is the story of well-known men and women and unnamed believers whose impact we will never know. Known and unknown, these first Christians left a legacy that every follower of Jesus would do well to follow. Reading their story is step one. Writing our own, by living and sharing the gospel, remains an ongoing challenge.

***

Going Deeper—Chapter 7

1. As you consider the birth of the church, it might be a good time to think about your relationship with a local church. What are your first memories of church? What is your favorite memory of church?
2. What is the significance of calling this chapter in the Story of God the Co-mission?
3. Recall some of the names by which the first believers in Jesus were known. Pick one and explain its meaning and significance.
4. *Navigating* outlines ten key events in Acts. How many can you name? Choose one and explain its importance.
5. Why was Paul such an important character in the story of the church?

Chapter 8: Letters to the Frontlines

Everyone enjoys receiving a letter, probably none more than a soldier away from home and facing an uncertain future. Anyone who has served in the military remembers the anticipation of mail calls. For the ordinary grunt, hunkered down in a bunker close to enemy lines, hearing from home provides a much-needed boost to morale. But if you were an officer on the frontlines, a written communique from headquarters took on added significance. A message from headquarters was often a matter of life and death.

We need to keep that picture front and center as we turn to our next section in the New Testament library. These twenty-one letters still fall in the Co-mission chapter of the Story of God. This part of the story began with the legacy of the first Christians recorded by Dr. Luke in the book known to us as the Acts of the Apostles.

Reading these letters should feel like looking over the shoulders of the earliest believers. In a way, we are reading someone else's mail. But in this case, the mail was addressed to churches and people just like us. They believed the same gospel. They faced the same struggles we and our churches confront every day. Most importantly, as we dive into these letters, we will quickly realize that none of them sound like casual notes between friends. Each reads like a vital communication between a "ranking officer," and the men and women huddled in the trenches within the sound of the battle, waiting for orders.

Churches as Battle Stations

Many of the letters were written to local churches. Think of a platoon of soldiers in the midst of a firefight. A few were addressed to individuals. Imagine a scout working his way behind enemy lines. All of the recipients of these letters were engaged in the battle. A civilian enjoying the comforts of home, far from the perils of the battlefield, would likely never appreciate instructions intended for those on the frontline. If we don't hear the rumble of the war, we won't understand the letters.

Few of us think of our churches that way. We are prone to regard our congregations as gatherings of old friends or spiritual retreats where we recharge our souls for the coming workweek. Not so those first Christians! For them, the local congregation was the "tip of the spear," the point of contact where heaven and hell collided. Each church was part of an invasion force taking the message of Jesus into enemy territory.

Writer Anne Dillard catches the spirit of these letters in her work, *Teaching a Stone to Talk.*[3] She says that churches are all too often like children playing on the floor with their chemistry sets, mixing up a batch of TNT to kill a Sunday morning. They haven't a clue what they are doing or the potential at their fingertips. Instead of ladies' hats, Dillard insists, church folk who really knew where they were would wear crash helmets. Ushers would issue life preservers and signal flares. They would lash us to our pews. Walking into a church is walking into a live battlefield!

Why We Need the Letters

The writers penned these letters to remind the readers that they were indeed on the frontlines. On one level, some might have thought they were simply a small social group that met on the back streets of the city to encourage one another in their new found faith. They were that. But they were so much more. They were a key component in God's strategy for overcoming the forces of evil in a world gone wrong. They were retaking lives held captive by the enemy. Their "secret weapon" was the empowerment of the Holy Spirit. Their only strategy is to talk about Jesus and live like Jesus! Their churches mattered because they were part of a battle bigger than themselves. Little has changed in two-thousand years. We still live on the frontlines. Our churches remain the "tip of the spear." These letters may not have been written to us, but they were written for us.

Letters Old and New

The format of these ancient letters differs significantly from their modern counterparts. In fact, few of us write letters any more. Emails and texts have replaced actual letters except in more formal or legal settings. Then, as now, letters followed a customary format. Even emails, texts, and other social media have their own accepted protocols. Students learned the letter format in their early education, just as most of us were taught letter writing in elementary school. We were instructed where to put the inside address, the date, the salutation, the closing, and the signature.

In the ancient world, a writer typically identified himself and the recipient in the opening lines. A blessing or good wishes followed the greeting. In these Christian letters, the blessing often comes in the form of a prayer. Depending on their relationship, the author might remind the readers of their past experiences together or their shared friendship before diving into the real reason for the letter. Generally, the letter would conclude with greetings to and from friends and associates known to both the writer and the recipient. Another blessing or prayer might be repeated at the very end. Most of the New Testament letters follow this or a very similar format. The term "epistle" is often used for some or all of these books. An epistle is simply another term for a letter, especially a more formal one.

The Authors of the Letters to the Frontline

To identify the author of a New Testament book, these letters included, scholars cite internal evidence and external evidence. Internal evidence would, of course, include the author's own self-identification. If the letter has no name attached to it, what and how he says what he does can provide clues as to who wrote it. External evidence would include the writings of early Christian historians and the traditions handed down from one generation to the next. This external testimony from second and third-century writers can be helpful but must always be evaluated with caution.

Based on the opening greeting, thirteen of the twenty-one letters come from the pen of Paul, two from Peter, one from James, one from Jude, and three from John. 1 John has no name attached, but because of the close similarity in style and content with the other two, most would attribute it to the same writer. Hebrews presents a more complicated problem. Early tradition attributed the book to Paul despite the fact that it is unsigned. Some early Christian commentators suggest it might have been written by someone else associated with Paul, such as Barnabas. Martin Luther proposed Apollos. The bottom line is that no one knows for sure.

This is not the place to discuss in detail the questions that are sometimes raised about the authorship of a few of the letters. Most often, critics point to differences in style and vocabulary as evidence that Paul, for example, couldn't have written all the books attributed to him. While some of these questions should be taken seriously, many of the differences can be explained by the fact that Paul sometimes used an associate who actually did the writing while he dictated. Different associates writing different letters could account for at least some dissimilarities in the letters. At other times, different topics might explain a different vocabulary and style.

Sorting the Letters to the Frontlines

Traditionally, these letters are divided into different categories according to when and why they were written. Four of Paul's letters were penned from prison—Ephesians, Philippians, Colossians, and Philemon. Understandably, Bible scholars call these the "prison epistles." 1 and 2 Timothy and Titus are labeled the "pastoral epistles" since they were addressed to men who were tasked with leading local congregations through difficult times. The books written by authors other than Paul are often lumped together as "general epistles." Also, these letters seem to be addressed to a wider audience than the letters of Paul that are intended for a particular congregation. Traditionally, Paul's letters are named for the recipients, the general epistles for the authors.

Why the Letters Were Written

The letters were written for a number of overlapping purposes, all related to equipping those on the frontlines for the various battles they faced. Generally, every letter was designed to encourage the Christian readers in their faith, whether addressed to a church or an individual. These early Christians often faced a hostile environment. New believers could understandably become discouraged. They needed reassurance that they had made the right decision in accepting

Christ. The writers often reminded them of all that Christ had done for them and the future hope he promised.

Some of the letters were designed to answer specific questions. 1 and 2 Corinthians, in particular, answer queries posed by various groups in the church. In Romans, Paul endeavors to clarify objections, or at least needed clarifications, about his teachings. The letters also often address specific situations or problems reported in the congregations. In his Corinthians correspondence, Paul offers pointed advice about divisions and moral lapses in that church reported to him by his associates. The Thessalonian letters seek to correct misunderstandings about the promised return of Christ. 2 and 3 John speak to personal problems and offers needed counsel to leaders in the church. Philemon, written to an individual, addresses a very specific situation.

Almost all of the letters seek to clarify the message of Jesus and its implications for the life of the church and Christian individuals. Galatians and Romans emphasize the priority of grace and the sacrifice of Jesus in contrast to the Jewish Law. Hebrews similarly explains the superiority of Christ's ministry with that of various aspects of the Jewish covenant. Colossians points to the all-sufficiency of Christ as an antidote to any who might claim that Jesus was only the first step toward a greater spirituality. The three pastoral epistles review the basics of the faith and offer young leaders needed insights. James, 1 Peter, and 1 John challenge believers to live their faith in practical ways.

In explaining the message of Jesus and applying it to life in various contexts, many of the letters emphasize the need to guard against false teachers who distort or outright deny the gospel. Galatians, Colossians, 2 Corinthians, Jude, 2 Peter, and the letters to

Timothy and Titus all emphasize this. The real danger develops, these letters insist, when false teachers show up inside the church. Some false teachers denied the identity of Jesus. Others added various rules or practices to the simple faith in Christ. Still, others undermined Christ's call to live holy and righteous lives. The church faced an ever-present temptation to contaminate the gospel with added rules or speculations. The letters all insist that the gospel provides the only effective antidote to false teachings.

Many of the letters always include personal expressions of appreciation for the support and prayers of the church. Philippians is very much a thank-you note from Paul, the missionary, to a congregation that had financially supported his ministry. 2 Corinthians includes an expression of gratitude for monies raised and an encouragement to complete the efforts to send aid to needy believers in Judea. Paul was passionate about creating a bond of love and support between his Gentile congregations and the Jewish churches.

The Warriors to Whom the Letters Were Written

The bulk of Paul's letters were addressed to churches that he had previously planted during his missionary travels. Romans is the exception. Paul wrote this letter to a church that he had never yet visited. The church knew him by reputation, and he obviously knew of the church. In some ways, it is an introduction to Paul's ministry in advance of a hoped-for visit. Four of his letters were addressed to individuals—Philemon, 1 and 2 Timothy, and Titus. In Philemon, Paul intercedes for a new convert. In the other three, he offers leadership guidance to associates he had sent to help local churches.

James, 1 and 2 Peter, Hebrews, Jude, and 1 John were addressed to wider audiences known to the author. Each offers instruction and guidance about how to apply the message of Jesus to their specific contexts. 2 and 3 John are more personal in nature. Both speak to specific individuals and the conflicts they faced living out their faith.

The Message to the Frontlines

What's the enduring message of these letters to the frontlines? Their message for us can be summarized in the following imperatives:

<u>Focus on the Message of Jesus</u>. All of the letters emphasize the centrality of the message of Jesus. James may be the one exception. James seems to echo the teachings of Jesus but only makes a passing reference to Christ himself and never mentions the cross and resurrection (James 1:1; 2:1). Most of the other letters remind their readers about what Christ has done for them and why they believe what they do about Jesus. The cross and the resurrection are at the center of the gospel. That must never be compromised. The letters explain the meaning of the gospel and contrast it with the false alternatives.

<u>Live Like You Believe the Message of Jesus</u>. Believing has implications. Committing to following Christ is a life-changing decision. Our identity determines our behavior. How we live, treat other people, and resist the temptations of the surrounding culture matters to the gospel. Believers should shine like lights in the darkness. We must be qualitatively different from the world around us. We are not alone in this challenge. The Holy Spirit empowers us from within. The teachings of Jesus point us in the right direction. Christian brothers and sisters support us in our struggles. In return, we support those around us.

<u>Love Like You Believe the Message of Jesus</u>. Christian unity and fellowship matter. Divisions or bickering between believers never furthers the gospel. They undermine it. Christian love offers the most powerful testimony to the reality of Christ in us. Christ has designed the church to function like different members of one body. We need not be alike. That's not God's plan at all. We differ for a reason. In love, we compliment each other. Our strengths fill our brothers' and sisters' weaknesses. In return, their strengths fill us. Likewise, Christian love expresses itself in practical ways. We encourage those who are discouraged. Out of love, Christians provide for the poor, care for the widow, and feed the hungry. Sharing out of love stands at the heart of who we are. We may not have always been that way, but Jesus changed us. We love one another and those in need because he loved us first.

<u>Share the Message of Jesus</u>. The gospel is meant to be given away. We are Christians because somebody told us about Jesus. We listened, the Holy Spirit convicted us, and we responded to it. Others deserve the same opportunity. They receive that opportunity when we tell the good news of Jesus to others. We know that it is not our good deeds that saved us. It was what Jesus did. We want others to see our lives and recognize a difference, but we also want them to know that the difference is because of Jesus. We proclaim him, not ourselves. Our churches reinforce what we believe about Jesus and help us learn to be more effective in taking that message to the world around us.

<u>Stay Strong Until Jesus Returns</u>. Followers of Jesus are people of hope. We live in dark times but look to a brighter day. Jesus is coming back. He will judge the living and the dead. No one knows when that day will be. That's why everyday matters. When he returns, our joy will more than overshadow the struggles and sacrifices. We live in the "in-between-times." Jesus came once as a sacrifice for sin. He will come again to receive those who eagerly wait for him. Waiting is hard. Sometimes, we become impatient. We are tempted to give up. But the believers who have gone before and those who stand beside us now keep us strong.

***

We may not look like warriors. Our church may not always act like battlestations. But that's exactly what we are! These letters to the frontlines remind us that we are in a battle. This is not a war that is fought with bullets and bombs. Ours is a spiritual struggle. The instructions the letters provide, the encouragement they offer, and the occasional two-by-four between the eyes are all intended to make us battle-ready. The message of Jesus, our lives of faithfulness to his teachings, and our devoted love for one another are what carry the day.

***

Going Deeper—Chapter 8

1.   This is strictly a personal opinion. How do you think the congregations you know best differ from those described in the New Testament?

2.   This might be a good time to review or learn for the first time the books of the New Testament and their order. How many can you name? Try to work on this for the next week.

3.   In general, what were the purposes of the New Testament letters?

4.   *Navigating* summarizes the message of the letters with four imperatives. Name these four imperatives and briefly explain each.

5. Why is it important for followers of Jesus to see themselves as warriors? What are some dangers of this perspective?

Chapter 9: The Grand Finale

Brad wasn't a total stranger to the Bible. His mother had sent him to Sunday School when he was little. He had heard the stories and remembered a few. But that was a long time ago. He hadn't thought much about it in years.

Brad still owned a Bible. In fact, he owned a couple. But he had never read much of either one. Then, one day, his indifference turned to curiosity. He opened the book and actually read several pages but soon lost interest. He thumbed through it a few times. Nothing caught his fancy. The Bible went back on the shelf and was soon covered with copies of old magazines. Out of sight, out of mind!

A few months later, Brad went through some hard times. He decided he would try the Bible again. He knew something was missing in his life. He thought fondly about those childhood memories of Sunday School and the joy he had found in the Bible. This time he decided on a different approach. He turned to the back of his Bible. He sometimes started books or magazines that way. He would go to the end first to get a feel for the direction of the story or the conclusion of the article before turning to the beginning. He thought that sounded like a good way to try the Bible.

When Brad started reading near the end of the Bible, he found himself smack dab in the middle of Revelation. To say it caught his attention would be an understatement. Suddenly, he was reading about fire-breathing dragons and multi-headed beasts. Stars were falling from the sky, and plagues were decimating the earth. Blood and death seemed to fill every page. Then the sky opened and a white knight came charging into the midst of a vast battlefield. Just as quickly, the scene changed to a giant city, streets of gold, and a garden paradise. What he was reading sounded important, but he couldn't make heads or tails of it. He kept reading. The more he read, the less he understood. His curiosity quickly turned to confusion.

Eventually, Brad turned to me for advice. He voiced his frustration with his attempts to understand the Bible. He wanted to know if he had made a mistake in starting at the back of the book. "How in the world could anyone make sense of this last book of the Bible?" he wondered out loud.

I suspect Brad is not the only person to become lost and confused in the wonders of Revelation. This last book may have caused almost as many potential Bible readers to throw in the towel as Leviticus, and that's saying something! Let's face it: Revelation is a difficult book. But it is an important book! It is also an appropriate book with which to end the Story of God. Revelation brings the whole Bible library to a fitting conclusion. I have attempted to capture the glory of this conclusion to the Bible by labeling the last chapter of the Story of God—The Coronation. This is the grand finale to which the whole of the Bible has been leading. But more than that, Revelation offers a blessing for those who read and obey its message (1:3). Although we may never fully understand all that the book contains, every effort in that direction will always prove worthwhile. That's a promise!

Beginning at the Beginning

Even veteran Bible readers sometimes misread the title of the book. This last book is called "Revelation" not "Revelations." The title is singular, not plural. The opening line describes what follows as the "revelation of Jesus Christ." That word describes something that is being "uncovered." What was previously hidden is now out in the open. That first line and title can cut two ways. "The revelation of Jesus Christ" can mean that Jesus is being revealed. No longer is he hidden. But that same phrase could mean that Jesus is revealing something that was once unknown. He is bringing it out into the open. Perhaps both are true.

Definitely, in one sense, the last book is a revelation about Jesus. At his first coming, he walked the earth as the "suffering servant." In the four gospels, many acknowledged him as Lord, but few viewed him as the King of Glory visiting his kingdom in disguise. But Revelation strips away the cover and reveals him for who he is. Imagine uncovering a new statue or a priceless painting. While the sheet remains in place, you can only see a vague outline of what is truly there. But when the time comes, the cloth falls away. Voila! There it is! No longer is the masterpiece hidden. The Great Reveal!

This last book reveals Jesus in three powerful, larger-than-life portraits. Each tells us something vital about our Lord. Revelation 1:12-15 presents the first portrait. The savior is pictured in a long robe with a golden sash across his chest. His eyes blaze like fire. His feet glow as burnished bronze fresh from the furnace. His voice thunders like a thousand breakers crashing against a rocky shore. He is amazing to behold! But most importantly, he is standing in the midst of the seven golden candlesticks, which, we are told, represent the churches to which Revelation is addressed. He is not absent. He is in the middle of what his people are facing.

The second portrait appears in Revelation 5:6-10. In chapter four, John looks into the very throne room of heaven. The Almighty is surrounded by all the creatures of heaven and earth, erupting in joyous worship. As chapter 5 opens, John notices that the right hand of the One on the throne holds a scroll. He instinctively knows that this scroll contains the secrets of the future John longs to know. A cry goes up that no one is able to unseal the scroll. John weeps in disappointment until he hears a new song. "Worthy is the Lamb." He sees a lamb slain, yet standing. The crucified and resurrected Christ! He is worthy! He alone, of everyone on heaven or earth, can unseal the scroll. Jesus is the key to the future of his people.

The last portrait comes near the end of the book—Revelation 19:11-16. Much has happened since the previous visions. We have finally arrived at the last battle. The forces of Satan and his allies have arrayed themselves against the Almighty and his people. Suddenly, the sky opens and a mighty rider on a white horse appears. He is called the Faithful and True. His eyes blaze with fire. Crowns adorn his head. His clothes drip with blood. His name—the Word of God. Out of his mouth comes a sharp sword. The righteous armies of heaven follow him into victory. He is the Lord of lords and King of kings!

When Christ is fully revealed for who he is, all will see him as the one who stands in the middle of his churches. He is with us. He will unfold our future. He knows what his people will face. And he is the victorious Lord who will guarantee our future victory!

This is a revelation of Jesus Christ. In another sense, and perhaps the main point of Revelation, the book contains mysteries that Jesus will unveil for us. This is something he alone can reveal. And what is that? He reveals the future, if not in detailed events, then in broad strokes that picture the ebb and flow of history and everything his people will face. Above all, he will unmask the Adversary and reveal him as he is, his tactics, and the ultimate defeat he is destined to face.

Most of us have seen the Hollywood portrayal of L. Frank Baum's classic story *The Wizard of Oz.* As the tale unfolds, Dorothy has been lifted from Kansas to a magical land filled with witches, munchkins, flying monkeys, and a powerful wizard who controls the fate of all who dwell in Oz. Dorothy and her dog Toto, joined by the Cowardly Lion, the Rusty Tin Woodsman, and the Brainless Scarecrow, head down the Yellow Brick Road to find the Emerald City where *The Wizard of Oz* holds court.

All four are convinced that only the Wizard can solve their dilemmas. Once in the palace of the Wizard, the quartet plus Toto are greeted by a vision of a huge head projected on the wall. They cower before the voice of the Wizard. Every terrible thing they have been told about the powerful Wizard must be true. He holds their fate in his hands.

Dorothy and the crew are frozen with fear. Toto, on the other hand, runs around barking uncontrollably. All efforts to quiet the little dog fail. Finally, an out-of-control Toto runs to a curtain on the other side of the room, tears at it with its teeth, yanking it to the floor. When the curtain falls, the frightened band sees not a giant wizard but a shriveled-up little old man pulling strings and speaking into a megaphone. Behold, the real *Wizard of Oz!* He was not nearly as frightening in real life as in the stories they had been told. The revelation of the Wizard!

The book of Revelation does for us what little Toto did for Dorothy and their friends. In Revelation, the Lord pulls back the curtain. He unveils the unseen so that heaven's reality, our future hope, and the true character of our enemy can finally be seen. The enemy is not nearly as invincible as he pretends to be. The Lord is even greater than we imagined. He is at work. That's all we need to know. He has it all under control. "Hallelujah! For our Lord God Almighty reigns" (19:6).

That's the ultimate revelation of Revelation!

A Special Type of Book

The uniqueness of Revelation also can make it hard to understand. It is unlike any other book in the New Testament library. Scholars call it a type of ancient literature known as apocalyptic. That term comes from the Greek word for revelation or uncovering. While Revelation is unique to the New Testament, it is not unique to the Bible or the ancient world. The Old Testament books of Daniel, Zechariah, and Ezekiel contain parts that read very much like this last book of the Bible. In fact, many of the same images in Revelation appear in these Old Testament books. Many other non-biblical books written during the period between the end of the Old and the beginning of the New Testament read much like parts of Revelation.

Apocalyptic literature typically contains vivid images and descriptions. The word pictures and symbolism sometimes served as a secret code that enabled the writer to communicate messages that only those on the inside would likely understand. Corrupt authorities often labeled such literature as subversive. These political leaders may not have always understood the meaning, but they knew they were being criticized. Revelation uses much of this kind of language. As a result, any attempt to interpret the images literally will miss the point. The grotesque images are meant to portray the horrible nature of the adversaries we face. The magnificent portrayals of Christ reflect his glory and power.

A part of this symbolism involves the use of numbers. The number of the antichrist is 666. The Spirit of God has seven eyes. The foundation of the heavenly city has twelve stones. Seven, in particular, holds a special place in Revelation. In fact, the entire book is organized around the number seven. For example, Revelation contains seven letters to seven churches, seven seals and seven trumpets, seven bowls, seven candlesticks, seven stars, seven angels, seven spirits, a lamb with seven horns and seven eyes, seven thunders, a red dragon with seven heads and seven crowns, a leopard-like beast with seven heads, a scarlet-colored beast with seven heads, seven mountains, seven kings. On and on the list could go.

Scholars tell us that many of these numbers had special significance in the ancient world. We use numbers in a similar way. Thirteen implies bad luck; seven good luck. For the ancient Jews, the number seven reflected the seven days of creation. It stood for something complete, total, and finished. Six, on the other hand, was incomplete. Three sixes was the ultimate evil. Twelve was a very spiritual number because of the twelve tribes of Israel, the foundation of the Jewish nation.

Apocalyptic literature often presents a behind-the-scenes perspective. On the surface, one reality exists. But underneath, another reality, the real story, can be found. But the two are connected. Evil may seem to rule the world, but the Lord still reigns! We just can't see all that he is doing. Revelation lifts the curtain and gives a peek at the movements of God, largely unseen through normal vision. It reveals the hand of God in history!

Like other writings of this type, Revelation defies comprehension if we insist on reading it in a linear fashion. If we read it from beginning to end, expecting that each section follows chronologically after the one before it, we will quickly find ourselves traveling in circles. Revelation contains countless interruptions to the storyline. Some are flashbacks. The action stops and our attention is taken back to something important that led up to this point. At other times, the vision is interrupted with a "flash up." Without warning, we are given a view of what is happening in heaven while the history we witness unfolds on earth. Sometimes, the story stops with a "flash down." A heavenly scene unfolds, only to suddenly shift back to earth. Any reader must proceed carefully and sometimes slowly in order to not miss the "flashes" in the story.

This kind of writing also emphasizes Last Things or eschatology. All apocalyptic literature majors in the end of the world or the conflict in the last days. Justice will come. Evil rulers and wickedness of every sort will eventually face condemnation. Judgment will put things right. God will finally turn the world right side up again. In a sense, Revelation is best read backward. At the very least, a reader will never appreciate the beginning and the middle without anticipating the end. We can endure the darkness because we know the light will break through before the conclusion of the story. For that reason, despite all the bloodshed and the extreme body count in Revelation, it remains a book of hope.

Four Views of This One Book

The unusual nature of Revelation and the human tendency to imagine that we know more than we really do about how God will draw this world to a conclusion has created multiple opinions about how to read this last book of the Bible. There seems to be no end to the speculations and conflicting perspectives. But many scholars whittle the options down to four general interpretive lenses through which Revelations is typically read.

The preterist view, from a Latin word meaning past, sees Revelation as a description of events that have already happened. Most often, those who read the book from this viewpoint understand the climactic judgment scenes of Revelation as a symbolic portrayal of the fall of Jerusalem and the cataclysm that befell the Jewish nation in AD 70.

The historicist view reads Revelation as a panoramic description of the history of the church from beginning to end. Some events are past; others are yet to come. The futurist view concentrates on the events leading up to the Last Days. All of the conflicts graphically outlined in the book are yet to happen, according to this perspective.

The idealist, on the other hand, views Revelation not as a detailed account of events past or future but as a symbolic review of the struggle between the forces of Satan and the people of God.

Countless hybrids and mutations of these four views abound. Personally, I am not convinced these four are mutually exclusive. Since I lean toward the idealist camp, I find things in Revelation that fit events that have already happened. I also think the book points to a grand cascade of activities yet to happen. My bottom line—I don't know what everything means in Revelation. I don't have to know. I know what matters. I know who is in control and I know the final outcome!

What We Know and Don't Know

This may be a good point to review a few basics about the End Times. Based not only on Revelation but also the teachings of Jesus and the rest of the New Testament (Matt 24-25; Mk 13; Lk 21; 1 Thess 4-5; 2 Thess 2-3; 1 Pt 4; 2 Pt 2-3; Jude), certain fundamental truths stand out.

We know that this world has an expiration date. Judgment will follow. The destiny of those "in Christ" has already been determined by the victory of Christ on the cross and resurrection. The outcome of the conflict between the forces of evil and the forces of righteousness is not in doubt. Spoiler alert: Jesus wins! But between now and then, the people of Christ will face tough times and tremendous opposition. That should not come as a surprise. Jesus promised as much.

On the other hand, some things remain unknown. God intends it that way. We don't know when the end will happen. Jesus said that it will come as a thief in the night. "No man knows the day or the hour," he insisted (Mt 24:42-44). Consequently, we don't know how long we have to persevere. The Lord calls us to prepare for the long haul yet live each day as if it were our last. That may be tough, but it is our assignment.

We also don't know the details about what will happen between now and the end. We know the kind of things to expect, just not the details. Much about the future, we don't know. But we know enough! Better yet, as the old hymn says, "We know who holds the future!"

Sadly, the landscape of history is littered with failed attempts to predict the Second Coming. Jesus said, "No man knows! Period!" Anyone who comes to Revelation looking for a calendar of the last days will always be disappointed. This last book offers little to encourage date setters. At the most, God has left signposts that point to the end. These are more on the order of warning signs to get our attention than specific events on a calendar. Ultimately, Revelation calls for "Son seekers" rather than "sign seekers." It asks us to believe that the Lord has everything under control and leave it at that! He alone keeps the calendar!

How the Story Ends

I will not pretend to know all the secrets to Revelation. But some things are clear and worth noting. First, a bit of background. According to the best sources, Revelation was written by John from the prison island of Patmos (a sort of Alcatraz just off the coast of what now is modern Turkey). The churches he knows best are in the midst of intense persecution. It is likely happening in the late 90's of the first century. Domitian ruled the Roman Empire. He is ruthless, sadistic, and determined to eliminate the troublesome Christians.

Many Romans viewed the Christians of the day as unpatriotic because they refused to worship the gods of the empire or the emperor himself. No one minds if Christians worship Jesus. That's their business, but they need to worship the national gods, too. This most Christians will not do. Jesus alone is Lord, they say. Many believers would die before the gladiators and beasts of the Coliseum rather than bow to another god.

In the midst of such darkness, persecuted believers cried out for God to intervene. The Lord responds with the visions of hope and comfort that John records. The Lord knows what's happening. He is still in control. When the time is right, and he alone knows when that will be, he will act. The evil rulers will be overthrown. The Evil One behind them will be destroyed once and for all. Best of all, the faithful will finally enter the glorious future the Lord has promised.

The first vision (chapter 1) presents the portrait of Christ among the churches. He is not absent or indifferent to the plight that his saints are facing. He is right there with them. Chapters 2 and 3 contain messages from Jesus to congregations in seven different cities. The cities and the churches were both real. But likely, the letters were intended to be read as representative of more than those seven congregations.

In these letters, the Lord identifies seven of the common challenges that his people of every age must confront. One church had fallen victim to the temptation to love something more than Jesus. A second faced the real likelihood of persecution and the temptation to abandon their faith for the sake of comfort and security. A third confronted the temptation to compromise with forces on the outside, another with corruption inside the church itself. Like many churches, another was tempted to live in the past on the residue of its reputation. The Lord offered a sixth congregation unlimited opportunities. It faced the decision to walk through an open door or remain satisfied with the status quo. The final church suffered the consequences of prosperity. It thought it needed nothing. In truth, it lacked everything that mattered. The solution for each was to humbly repent before the Lord. Only in him would they realize their hopes and dreams.

In chapter 4, the scene shifts to heaven. John sees the throne of God and a seven-sealed scroll that contains the future of his people. Only the lamb is worthy to open the scroll (chapter 5). In chapter 6, the seven seals are lifted one by one. Each reveals the conditions that believers will confront in the future. With the opening of the last seal, seven trumpets herald a louder and louder warning of pending doom on Earth. Think of the seals as a tornado watch, a call to be on the alert. The trumpets are like the tornado warning. It's time to take cover. In Revelation, despite the warnings, most refuse to turn to God in repentance (6:15-17; 9:20-21).

The vision switches back and forth between heaven and earth. Martyred saints ask, "How long, O Lord, how long?" As the final trumpet sounds, Judgment Day has arrived. Before the final act, the vision flashes back to a panoramic review of the ongoing battle between the Adversary and the people of God (12-14). In chapter 15, the Lord finally says enough is enough. He sends forth angels with seven bowls of wrath (16).

Heaven announces the ultimate downfall of Satan and his allies (17-18). But he will not go down without a fight. In his final death tremors, the great Dragon (Satan) wages war against the saints of God. The warrior on the white horse arrives. Victory is won! The Lord God Omnipotent reigns (19:6)! Invitations are issued for the Wedding Feast of the Lamb and the grand coronation. Eventually, Satan and his forces are dealt with once and for all. Those whose names have been written in the Book of Life and washed in the blood of the lamb are ushered into the promised paradise as the New Heaven and the New Earth become reality for all eternity.

Revelation is a book of hope and promise. It is the story of the God who is faithful and true. He has promised life in his Son. He has promised reward and blessing to all who are "in Christ." He has promised judgment and justice for the wickedness that seems to prevail at times. Revelation tells the story of how God keeps his word. It won't always be easy. It is sometimes not a pretty picture. It may not follow the timetable we imagine. At times, we will wonder what's taking the Lord so long. But he has it all under control. When the time is right, he will act.

A Parting Word

The literary giant T. S. Eliot ends his poem of despair, *The Hollow Men*[5], with the lament, "This is the way the world ends, not with a bang but a whimper." Elliot was wrong! It ends with the sound of a trumpet!

As Paul describes this last chapter of the Story of God, "For the Lord himself will come down from heaven, with a loud command, with the voice of the archangel and with the trumpet call of God, and the dead in Christ will rise first. After that, we who are still alive and are left will be caught up together with them in the clouds to meet the Lord in the air. And so we will be with the Lord forever. Therefore encourage one another with these words" (1 Thess 4:16-18).

A man vacationing at a resort high in the Swiss Alps awoke to what he knew was the sound of an earthquake. He jumped out of bed, threw on his clothes, and ran down the stairs. He rushed to the front desk and asked the clerk what he needed to do. The noise sounded like the mountains were breaking up. He was understandably scared. The older clerk at the desk calmly explained, "Sir, we are on the West side of the mountain. As the sun comes up in the East, the snow and ice expand as they begin to warm the earth. The expansion causes that crashing noise. It's not the end of the world. It's the beginning of a new day."

Believer, that noise you hear or those headlines you read may be signaling the Last Days. Only the Lord knows for sure. But this we do know. It's not really the end of the world. It's the beginning of a New Day!

***

Going Deeper—Chapter 9

1. What has been your experience with the Book of Revelation? Do you think of this book positively, negatively, or just confusing? Why?
2. What are some of the ways Jesus Christ is described in Revelation? Which do you consider the most significant? Why?
3. How does that climactic scene in *The Wizard of Oz* illustrate the main theme of Revelation?
4. What kind of literature is Revelation? Why is this important for understanding the book?
5. What is your favorite part of the book of Revelation? Why?

Chapter 10: Confessions of a Bible Reader

I remember receiving my first Bible years ago. I hugged it close to my chest all the way home from the store. I kept it in my bedroom during the week and carried it to church on Sundays. Even though I was young, I knew that the Bible was an important book.

That King James Version Bible with the black cardboard cover wasn't the only one I owned. I will never forget that small New Testament the Gideons presented to my class at school. For years, I carried it in my back pocket almost everywhere I went. Later, an aunt gave me an expensive leather-bound Bible for my high school commencement. It was beautiful. Eventually, I graduated from owning a Bible to reading it.

I don't remember when I first started really reading the Bible. I am sure I read it at least occasionally during those early years. As a teenager and as a young adult, the Bible became a more important part of my life. Eventually, I read the entire book. It took a while, certainly months, quite possibly even longer. Through my college years, marriage, and starting a family, I continued to read it. At some point, I committed to reading it regularly and at a pace that would take me through it every year. I quickly learned that reading the Bible from cover to cover in a year takes about fifteen to twenty minutes a day. I have also learned that skipping a day or two can be hard to make up! Years later, I have read the Bible through many times.

The big question is: why? Why do I read the Bible over and over again? I don't normally read other books, even ones that I enjoy, a second or third time, much less repeatedly over the years. Why do I continue to read the Bible?

I am sure, at this point, it is partly out of habit. It becomes second nature. My Bible reading habit began the day I consciously made the decision to read it as close to daily as I could. I have done so for years. I don't even think about it anymore. I miss it when I don't.

I suppose another explanation for my Bible-reading habit is the simple fact that I am a reader. I enjoy reading. I did as a child, and I still do today. I know not everyone does. To me, it is sad to hear adults, especially grown men, announce proudly that they haven't cracked a book since high school. It is especially lamentable to hear Christians make that claim when I suspect that, in too many cases, the neglect includes the scriptures. In reality, the person who doesn't read differs little from the person who cannot read. It need not be that way.

Today, even poor readers and those with impaired vision can still "read" the Bible by listening to the recorded versions that are available online, many free. Also, Bibles are readily available in large print formats, in countless translations, and even in Braille.

I Don't Read the Bible Because

Let me make it clear. I don't read the Bible because I have to. No one forces me to read. I am not completing an assignment for school or work. No one checks up on me. Nor do I read it because I think it is a requirement for salvation, as if reading the Bible somehow qualifies me for heaven or for at least first-class accommodations. I don't even believe that Bible reading in and of itself is a measure of spiritual maturity. Don't get me wrong. Reading the Bible certainly contributes to spiritual growth. But obedience, not notches on my Bible, is the better mark of maturity.

I also don't read the Bible because I understand everything in it. If I had quit reading scripture the first time, I came across something that puzzled me, I would have stopped long ago. Certainly, the more I read, the more I understand. But I still encounter passages that leave me scratching my head. I keep reading because what I do understand far outweighs the parts I don't. That's true quantitatively, but more importantly, qualitatively. Not all parts of the Bible are of equal importance. I try not to become stuck in the minors at the expense of the majors.

This leads to another false motive for reading the Bible. I don't read it because I worship it. The Bible is not my God. It is not an idol or an object of superstition. It can be. I need to keep the distinction clear. I don't venerate the Bible or feel obliged to treat it with "kid gloves" as if dropping it or somehow soiling it convicted me of blasphemy. Just carrying a copy doesn't shield a person from dangers or demons. However, I have heard of a few instances where a well-placed Bible in a soldier's shirt stopped a bullet. I suspect there have been times in my life when I have tread dangerously close to the line separating grateful appreciation and idolatrous worship of the Bible. I have hopefully learned to distinguish between my Lord and the book that he made possible.

I also hope I have learned to read the Bible for reasons other than fashioning a club. All too often, I have searched the scriptures to find just the right "clobber verse" with which to beat someone over the head in a religious argument. Truth matters! But so does motive. When I read my Bible in order to point out someone else's mistakes,

I am likely to overlook my own. The "log in my own eye" can easily overshadow my neighbor's "speck." Hopefully, I have learned to no longer view the Bible as the exclusive possession of my church, my tribe, or my denomination. My opinions, speculations, and deductions do not define orthodoxy. Pretending that they do leads to dark and ugly places.

I can also think of a few reasons that are probably, in and of themselves, not bad but aren't really my best motives. For example, I don't read the Bible because of its enormous cultural value. Probably, no book has affected the English language and Western culture as much as the Bible. Reading it will help make a person better educated and more culturally aware. But I don't read it in order to prepare for my big break on *Jeopardy*. Similarly, I don't read it for its historical information or literary value. Nor is it primarily a source of good advice. The Bible contains all of this—valuable history, great literature, and wise advice. But that is not enough to keep me coming back again and again.

I Read the Bible Because

Why do I read my Bible? The reasons are many. But the most important thing is that it led me to Jesus. It contains the words of life. The gospel, *His Story*, convicted me of sin, turned my heart toward God, and brought me to the feet of the Savior who bore my sins on the cross. I can read the Bible as an end in itself, but that is never enough. As Jesus warned the religious leaders of his day, "You study the Scriptures diligently because you think that in them you have eternal life. These are the very Scriptures that testify about me, yet you refuse to come to me to have life" (Jn 5:39-40).

My parents, my childhood church, the preacher who first shared the gospel with me, and countless others used the Bible to point me to Jesus. But they always emphasized that the Savior was Christ, not the book. To reverse that order would be like stopping at the roadside sign rather than continuing on to view Niagara Falls.

I read the Bible because, through it, I receive a better understanding of my Lord and his plans. Paul contended that those who read what he had written would "be able to understand my insight into the mystery of Christ, which was not made known to people in other generations as it has now been revealed by the Spirit to God's holy apostles and prophets" (Eph 3:4-5). No place else offers more insight into the will of God. The Bible helps me comprehend what he is doing in my world and my life. I like C. S. Lewis' analogy. "I believe that the sun has risen: not only because I see it, but because by it I see everything else."[5] The Bible brings my God and my world into focus.

The Bible has done so much in my life. It has shaped my thinking, convicted me of foolish mistakes, set me on a better course, and made me more and more into a man of God. I shudder to think who I would be or the shape of my life were it not for the direction of God's Word. It, indeed, has been "a lamp for my feet, a light on my path" (Ps 119:105). I haven't always made the right decisions or walked the "straight and narrow." But the scriptures have never failed to point the way out of the wilderness and direct me back toward the center of God's will.

Through reading the Bible, I have also found hope. So many voices in our world spread discouragement and despair. Everywhere I turn, I see evil men triumph and good people suffer. I could easily doubt my future or the futures of the ones I love. My world offers more than enough reasons to give up. That's when I need the reminder that "everything that was written in the past was written to teach us so that through the endurance taught in the Scriptures and the encouragement they provide we might have hope" (Rom 15:4). It is not just a light at the end of the tunnel I see, but the "light of the world." I am reminded again and again that even when everything seems out of control, it isn't. My God is in control!

I also read the Bible because of the amazing community of people it builds around me. I regularly worship with other believers. We sing. We pray. We support and encourage each other. We also read and study the Bible together. I can and do read the Bible on my own. But something special happens when I do it in concert with others.

Sometimes, studying the Bible with others might seem like a waste of time. I don't always benefit in the way I think I should. Some of what I hear is far from edifying. But it still matters because of the people it brings into my life. Young and old, educated and those not so much, those new to the faith and veterans all gather for a common purpose. They want to know their God better and think his thoughts after him. A common pursuit of the Bible makes that possible. The people around me make me a better follower of Jesus.

I can't read the Bible for long without remembering my parents and grandparents. None of them were blessed with the educational opportunities I have had. But they loved the Lord and they loved his book. I doubt if any of them had ever read the Bible as thoroughly or mastered its details to the extent that many have, but they read it and they cherished it. They learned from what others could teach them about it. And they endeavored to live by its teachings to the best of their ability. Most of all, they believed in its Author.

Ultimately, I suppose I continue to read the Bible day after day, year after year because I find in it a joy and satisfaction that I have found nowhere else in life. I read it. I study it. I meditate on it. Through it, God speaks to me. The Bible feeds my soul! I am convinced anyone can discover those same riches in the pages of the Bible. As Psalm 19 declares, "They are more precious than gold, than much pure gold; they are sweeter than honey; than honey from the honeycomb. By them your servant is warned; In keeping them there is great reward" (Vv. 10-11).

***

Going Deeper—Chapter 10

1. When did you first start seriously reading the Bible? What do you recall about that?

2. How has your experience of reading the Bible changed your life?

3. What are a few bad reasons for reading the Bible?

4. What do you consider your biggest reason for reading the Bible?

5. What goal would you set for your Bible reading for the next year?

Appendix 1: How to Study the Bible

Reading the Bible promises countless blessings. Reading it regularly and consistently multiplies those benefits. But one additional step can take the Bible reader to a whole new level. Eventually, reading the Bible needs to develop into studying the Bible. What's the difference? The two obviously walk hand in hand.

Reading it thoughtfully always involves a measure of study. To the extent that the two can be separated, I would define the first step as the process of casually reading for the purpose of understanding the big picture and the flow of the story. Study, however, requires slowing down, looking for the details, and grasping the context and connections of the passage with those before and after it. Studying becomes the natural extension of reading carefully.

Reading can sometimes be quick and superficial, especially when keeping pace with a Bible-in-a-year reading plan. Study always demands more. Bible study pursues three goals—information, inspiration, and transformation. All three are vital.

The Bible provides us with tremendous amounts of information. The people, places, and events matter. But we can easily become lost in the facts and never discover the real treasure. The Lord intends scripture to touch the heart as well as the head. It affects our will, our intentions, and our priorities. This leads quite naturally to the third step—transformation. If we truly pay attention to what we read and study, it will change our behavior. God's Word moves from our head, through our hearts, and into our hands.

Moving from reading to studying also requires a few tools. Obviously, you need a Bible. I recommend a sturdy Bible with paper that can handle marking and taking notes. For Bible study, you will need a pen or pencil. If you intend to write in your Bible, test the pen first. You won't want your notes to bleed through to the other side of the page or fade, becoming hard to read later. A good notebook is another essential. Hopefully, you will want to keep track of your thoughts as you study or note questions that you want to pursue in the future. Where you study, just as where you regularly read the Bible, can affect the process. A quiet, comfortable (but not too comfortable!) chair and desk or table will invite you back again and again. Too many distractions will sabotage the best intentions.

One other preliminary may be necessary to acknowledge before we dive into our Bible study. Unfortunately, we sometimes have to unlearn some of the lessons we've been taught by our past experiences for what passes as Bible study, especially group study. Too often, Sunday School and small groups have trained us to believe that Bible study means reading a passage of scripture and asking the questions: How do I feel about this passage? What do I think about this passage? What does this passage mean to me?

These might be questions we may want to ask eventually. But they should not be the first questions, or certainly not the only questions we ask. If they are, we are probably looking at our own reflections in a mirror rather than actually studying the words of the Bible on the page in front of us!

Instead of asking how we feel about the passage, we need to ask, in this order: What does it say? What does it mean? What should I do? For many of us, this process may require us to retrain ourselves to focus on the actual passage of the Bible that we are studying. Our urge to explore our own thoughts and feelings must be temporarily tamed.

To keep the Bible study experience as concise as possible without making it too simplistic, I break the process into six steps. The four core actions form the word R.E.A.D. To these, I have added two bookends that are indispensable to Bible study. Many veteran believers instinctively practice most of this. For them, this may be a review. I think in terms of R.E.A.D. But first things first—

Step One: Pray. Prayer forms the first bookend. We can read the Bible like we read the newspaper or a novel, but if we do, we make a big mistake. If you believe as I do that the Bible is a special word from God, then we dare not approach it arrogantly, thinking we can figure it out on our own. To get the most from our Bibles, we must humbly come within "hearing distance." We never do that better than when we pray, admit our limitations, and ask for the ultimate Author's assistance.

Step Two: Read. Reading with focus can be hard. Sometimes, when I open my Bible, my eyes move across the page, but my mind is elsewhere. I might be reviewing what I saw the last time I read that particular passage. At other times, I hear the voice of a favorite preacher or Bible teacher telling me what I should conclude from the passage.

To actually read, I need to slow down and concentrate as if I were reading it for the first time. I often read a passage that I am studying from at least a couple of different translations: my normal Bible and one that I don't know as well. The unfamiliar wording or phrasing of a seldom-read translation helps me to see fresh thoughts. In this context, I define a passage as at least a paragraph and no more than a chapter. I want the section I am studying to be manageable enough that I can give it my full attention.

Step Three: Examine. Reading can degenerate into scanning. To truly read for study means taking the time to see the details. I can get the big picture easily enough, but I want more. I start with *the basics*: who, when, where, what, why, and how? At this point, I started taking notes. Next, I look for keywords, repeated words, important phrases, or ideas in the passage. I often circle or underline these in my Bible. I next focus on "signpost" words or phrases, words such as—in order to, because of, therefore, however, but, or finally. Each signals the writer's thoughts.

Step Four: Analyze. Here, I bring these various threads together. First, I write a brief summary of the passage in my own words. This obviously involves my notebook. I make a list of the main or most important ideas in the passage or the lessons the writer seems to be trying to communicate. Of course, I want to pay attention to the surrounding context. As Bible teachers say, "A text without a context is simply a pretext to make the text say whatever you want."

My analysis can go as deep and wide as my time and interest allow. At some point, I may consult Bible dictionaries, commentaries or other helps. I can use a concordance to find similar passages, always keeping context in mind. Above all, I must resist the temptation to go to outside sources too quickly. They will simply undermine my own attempts to study the Bible.

Step Five: Do. Bible study is not for mere amusement or the accumulation of Bible trivia. In the final analysis, I read the Bible to better understand the will of God for my life. I know that not all of the Bible was written *to* me, but it was written *for me*. The Lord intends me to learn from and put into practice what I study. I write in my notebook the answers to such questions as: What *facts* to be believed do I find in the passage? What *commands* are to be obeyed? What *instructions, warnings, or examples* to be heeded do I need to note? What *promises* to be received do I find? What *resolutions* should I make as a result of what I have discovered?

<u>Step Six: Pray Again.</u> This is the other bookend. I end where I started, seeking the mind and the blessing of the heavenly Father. Only as his Spirit guides me will I truly benefit from his word. I ask for opportunities to put into practice what I have learned. I confess the sin my study has exposed. I pray for people who have come to mind as I read. I thank my God for the new blessings I have recognized.

***

Bible study always involves a learning curve. At first, the process may seem artificial and tedious. But the more you study the Bible, the more comfortable you will become with it. Think of it as training experience. The first time you began learning a new skill or preparing for a physical goal, you were easily discouraged. You were probably tempted to give up. But persistence always pays off. Allow yourself room to grow and improve in this area as well.

Don't overthink what you are doing. This isn't an assignment for school. No one is going to grade your notes. This is all about learning to think about the actual words of scripture. The deeper you reflect on God's Word, the more your faith will grow. The blessings will multiply. Soon, you find your faith, hope and love overflowing into the lives of others. That's the goal of Bible study—to know, love, and serve the Lord more faithfully.

***

Going Deeper—Appendix 1

1. Practice the principles of How to Study the Bible using the tiny book of Philemon.

2. What's the main storyline of Philemon? Who are the main characters?

3. What applications to your life do you find in Philemon?

Appendix 2: How to Teach the Bible

Clearly, not everyone can or should be a teacher. But those who are should be prepared and effective. A teacher needs to know the subject, in this case, the Bible. But a teacher also needs to understand how students learn and how to recognize when real learning has taken place.

Here, I am thinking primarily about adult learning. Teaching children or youth may share some of the same principles, but that's not our main concern in what follows. Also, this discussion will focus on a group setting. It might be a Sunday school class, a small group, or a few friends gathered for a regular informal coffee klatsch.

But to be a "Bible teaching" occasion, the group must be intentional (have an agreed upon purpose), involve at least some study of the Bible, and have an acknowledged leader. The leadership may be formal or informal. In a typical church, leadership/teaching is often shared or rotated. Such gatherings are almost always voluntary. No one is forced to attend or graded on their performance. Also, the most effective church groups are multidimensional. They gather for learning but also for fellowship, service, and prayer.

How Adults Learn

Many Bible study groups flounder and eventually fade away due to a lack of clarity about how adults learn in a voluntary setting. Some still contend that the best learning happens when a knowledgeable, prepared teacher stands before a group and lectures. This practice imagines that teaching simply involves placing a funnel in the student's ear and pouring in the information. In a formal classroom, maybe; but seldom in a volunteer setting! More often, if the information goes in that one ear, it just as quickly flows out the other. Adult Bible learning involves more than just the transfer of information. Just as with Bible study, Bible teaching has three goals: information, inspiration, and transformation (see Appendix 1). How we teach must recognize all three.

Whether they know it or not, most adults are "just-in-time" learners. They pursue knowledge that they deem important and practical. Abstract and theoretical topics are tolerated only as long as the student sees a way to translate that knowledge into his or her life. This doesn't mean the study is simplistic or superficial. It does mean that when I teach the Bible, I need to ask the question "why" as well as "what." If I can't verbalize how I expect students to practice on Monday what I am teaching on Sunday, then I am not prepared to teach.

Also, adult learning in the typical church setting is caught more than it is taught. That is to say, a student learns from what the teacher says but also from how the teacher says it and how others in the group respond. Spiritual growth happens when students see someone they admire voicing and exhibiting something they want. A student yearns to hear not only the leader but also his or her peers express the principles of the faith and how it relates to life. Relevant group participation matters.

Focusing on the content of the Bible remains vital. Without it, discussion devolves into empty, meaningless chatter. One of the leader's most important roles is to encourage honest, thoughtful, and relevant discussion. At the same time, the leader must discourage superficial, irrelevant, or mean-spirited comments and discussion. This is no simple task. The person in charge teaches Christian character and values by how he or she guides and redirects the group, especially during times of disagreement or conflict.

How Teachers Teach

Let's start with the assumption that the leader has studied the biblical material to be taught. A discussion guide, workbook, or full-blown curriculum lesson plan does not substitute for personal study of the assigned scripture. Having studied the passage on his own, the teacher must still decide how to present the material to the class in an engaging, relevant way. The task is far from easy. The possibilities are endless.

Years ago, veteran Christian educator Lawrence O. Richards[6] developed a popular and effective approach to Bible teaching that emphasizes content and participation. Others have offered countless variations on his original plan. The principles are sound, easily adaptable, and worth the effort required to apply them to the typical small group or Sunday school class setting. Many published curriculum guides or small group lesson books adopt some form of Richards' approach. Richards organized his suggested lesson plan around a four-step process that he described with four words: *hook, book, look, and took*. All four are important; balancing the four is critical.

Hook—A teacher has only one chance to make a first impression. How the class/group begins will often determine how it progresses. The first step is to arouse the group's interest while steering them toward the "big idea" of the lesson. This can be accomplished in countless ways—relating a personal experience, telling a story, citing a current event, or a thought-provoking question that prompts discussion. The hook must be brief and on topic. It must form a natural bridge to the main subject of the biblical lesson. In the typical forty-five-minute to hour class, the *hook* should take up no more than ten minutes. Longer meeting sessions will allow for more time spent on this opening step.

Book—This is the heart of the lesson. The focus turns to the biblical material. The teacher can summarize the background and context of the passage. A participant can read the text itself. The teacher then guides the class through the main ideas of the scripture. The questions involved in personal Bible study (Appendix 1) can be used to help the group analyze and understand the main ideas of the passage. The teacher can model and teach good Bible study practices during this time.

In a larger group and where the meeting space allows, the class can divide into smaller sub-groups to complete a portion of the study of the passage. The sub-group can then report back to the whole group. The more involvement, the better. A well-prepared teacher will vary the kinds of group activities that are used from week to week. In a well-balanced lesson, the *Book* portion should consume about a third of the group's time.

Look—After thinking through the passage, the class can then turn to application. The *Book* must come before the *Look*! What would life look like if the "big idea" of the text were put into practice? The questions from the *Do* section of the R.E.A.D. Bible study format (Appendix 1) will work for this purpose. Discussion matters at this point. Everyone should be encouraged to contribute, but the teacher needs to keep the conversation focused on the application of the text and not allow it to stray into unrelated areas. This application process might involve ten to, at the most, fifteen minutes of the session.

Took—This is the grand finale. In a class, the most memorable parts will most often be the beginning and the end. Students should leave with some aspect of the "big idea" on their minds. The leader can summarize the lessons learned, the highpoints of the discussion, and/or note a particular challenge for the coming week. At its best, the group can together develop an agreed-upon action that each person will endeavor to complete by the next meeting. The best *Took* will tie back to the *Hook* with which the class began. This will last no more than five minutes.

No Easy Road

Make no mistake about it: this approach to leading a group or class requires preparation and work on the part of the teacher. Guiding relevant discussion and leading students into personal discovery through appropriate Bible study practices is not a simple task. The leader must study, pray, and think through the questions that can lead to profitable discussion. She must remember that her actions will teach as much as her words.

Teaching the Bible provides the kind of reward that can be found in a few other places. Of course, everyone knows the teacher always learns more than the student. But beyond that, the teacher is privileged to see students grow in their faith, learn new truths, and hopefully adopt better ways of living out their faith in everyday life. That's the goal of effective Bible teaching—information, inspiration, and transformation!

***

Going Deeper—Appendix 2

1.   Outline a brief lesson plan for a small group or class on Philemon using the principles of *How to Teach the Bible.*

2.   Write a *Hook* question with which you might start the group discussion.

3.   Outline the main teaching points (*Book*) that you would want to emphasize in the lesson.

Appendix 3: Sharing Our Faith

Sharing our faith with others is a privilege, not a duty. The difference and the attitude that goes with it will determine everything about our efforts. Telling friends and family about what we have learned in our journey through the Bible is a natural overflow of our growing faith. Joy is contagious. Others notice it and want to know where it comes from. On the other hand, any dread we have about talking about our faith will push people away. Others will sense it in our lives and want nothing to do with our faith, regardless of what we may claim to the contrary.

This is the spirit of the Bible's appeal for us to point others to Jesus. "But in your hearts revere Christ as Lord. Always be prepared to give an answer to everyone who asks you to give the reason for the hope that you have. But do this with gentleness and respect . . ." (1 Peter 3:15). Our message about Christ radiates from a place of hope and love, never from harshness or condemnation.

Telling Our Story of Hope

Any effort to share our faith begins with our own testimony. I recommend writing out your personal story on paper. Once you have worked through this process, you will be better able to share with a friend what Christ has done for you. This account should be brief (just five to ten minutes at the most), honest, and positive. Tell what your life was like before Jesus. Explain the difference Jesus has made. Don't over-glorify the past or the present. Tell how you came to faith, who influenced you, and what you were told. If you became a Christian as a child, emphasize what Jesus has done in your life to change and grow you in the years that followed.

Pray for Opportunities

With your own journey of faith clearly in mind, you can now ask the Lord to send someone across your path who needs to hear your story. Ask the Lord to open your eyes to recognize the person he sends your way. Pray that you will have the courage to speak, the wisdom to know what to say, and the grace to speak without sounding self-righteous. Above all, ask the Lord to help you be gentle, kind, and Christ-like.

Building Bridges of Hope

Most opportunities to share our faith will grow out of friendships. Those who have yet to come to faith are seldom interested in anything we have to say about Christ until they have come within the "caring and hearing distance" of our hearts. We can proactively seek such relationships by listening, showing genuine interest in those we know, asking questions that provide them an opportunity to tell us who they are and what they care about, and, of course, giving them our undivided attention. We can look for ways to bless them by meeting a practical need. This works both ways. Others will grow closer to us as we allow them to meet our needs in our lives. Of course, as opportunities arise, we can invite friends to join us in worship or for some special occasion at our church. Growing churches find ways to create activities that encourage such invitations.

Moving Across the Bridge

Ultimately, we want to transition the friendship to an opportunity to talk about our faith. This assumes that the friendship is not just a tactic designed to turn the friend into a target. Others can smell such a betrayal from a mile away. Friendships that become gospel opportunities take time, sometimes years! Gentle patience and loving prayer can melt the hardest heart.

Opportunities to share our story may come in bits and pieces through normal conversation. If at all possible, these tidbits of faith need to spotlight Jesus, not the church, hope, not negativity and love, not condemnation. Above all, we never want to take a negative response from our friend as personal or final. Often, the first reaction is a test. The friend wants to know if our friendship is genuine and if we are "safe" to talk with about deeply personal matters.

At some point in our friendships, we may be blessed with the opportunity to openly share the gospel. That's what we have been praying for. It might come in the form of a question about a spiritual concern or the sharing of a personal problem. Whenever the opportunity arises, we need to seize the moment. Thinking through our explanation of the gospel ahead of time will help ensure we are ready when our friend is ready.

A helpful key that can unlock the door to sharing the gospel with a friend is to ask a clarifying question. The right question can prompt the friend to think through what he actually already believes. One helpful way to do this was offered by the late D. James Kennedy in his once-popular work *Evangelism Explosion*.[7] Kennedy suggested asking, at the appropriate time, the question, "What do you think you would say if you were to stand before the Lord today and he would ask you, 'Why should I let you into my heaven?'"

The answer reveals for us where our friend stands in his relationship with God. Also, as the friend thinks through their own answer, he may better appreciate the promise of the gospel when we begin to explain it to him. The answer can be followed by a permission question—Can I share with you what I have learned from the Bible about answering that important question? A positive answer provides the green light we need to begin an explanation of the hope we have in Christ (1 Pt 3:15).

Sharing the Good News of Jesus with Clarity

How we explain our faith can take many forms, but it will always include certain key truths. Our message needs to be a clear, concise, systematic presentation of Jesus in a way that makes sense to a person who may not share our faith. Thinking through what we would say ahead of time is the only way to be prepared when the Lord opens the door.

The following example outlines one simple, Bible-based approach to explaining the gospel of Jesus. John 3:16 offers a practical entry point into the gospel. Most people, even those who know little else about Jesus, have heard this familiar verse. [If possible, open a Bible to this verse and read it to your friend or ask your friend to read it.]

First and foremost, our faith starts with God. [Circle the word *God* in the verse.] God is God! God is the maker of all that exists. The Bible says he is powerful and personal. He made us and loves us beyond anything we can imagine. [Circle *love* in the verse.] And he also made us with a yearning for him. St. Augustine famously prayed, "You have made us for yourself, O Lord and our hearts are restless until they rest in you."[8] [Romans 1:19-20 might prove helpful.]

[Circle the word *world* in John 3:16.] We are part of that world God loves. The Bible tells us that despite God's love for us, we have all sinned. In the simplest terms, that means we have tried to live our lives without him. We have ignored God. More than that, we have disobeyed his standards by doing what we shouldn't or not doing what we should. That attitude and those actions separate us from God, enslave us in destructive patterns of behavior, and will finally destroy us. That's the meaning of *perish* in John 3:16. [Romans 3:23, 5:6-11, and 6:23 can help.]

But the good news is that God has done for us what we couldn't do ourselves. We have separated ourselves from God's best for us, but he built a bridge from his side to ours. [You can illustrate this by drawing a divide with God on one side and the world on the other and a cross-shaped bridge spanning the rift.]

Our Heavenly Father did this in Jesus Christ, who came to earth as God in the flesh to show us the way to God, demonstrate his perfect love, and finally die on the cross for our sins and conquer death by his resurrection from the grave. [Underline *gave* and *his one and only son* in John 3:16.] The message of Jesus, the life that he lived, and the hope that he provides through the cross and the resurrection offers us hope. That hope promises the forgiveness of our sins, life beyond the grave, and a place prepared for us in God's heaven. [Circle *eternal life* in the verse.]

[Point to the words *whoever believes in him* in John 3:16.] God has built the bridge across the separation between his love and our lives. We can't cross it by our own efforts or good deeds. We can only move across the bridge to that new life by declaring our willingness to leave what has separated us from him, move toward trust in what he offers, and invite him to change us from the inside out. It is only by his love and grace that we can move into that life.

The beloved verse brings us to the fork in the road. Which direction we go determines everything. [You might read John 3:17-18 at this point. Added biblical information might include Romans 10:9-10, 1 John 1:8-2:2 and Acts 2:36-38.]

Asking for their response to what you have shared naturally follows. We might ask, "Do you understand? Do you have any questions? Are you willing to take the step of acknowledging Christ and asking him into your life?" Once the person has indicated a desire to accept Christ's invitation, it is totally appropriate to bow in prayer with our friend and encourage him to tell the Father Almighty the desire of his heart. If the person is reluctant, we encourage them. If he insists he is not ready, we don't give up. We take a couple of steps back and patiently encourage, teach, and, of course, pray.

Once our friend has heard and accepted the message of who Jesus is and what he has done for us on the cross and in his resurrection, he or she is ready to take the next step. Until the person has comprehended the message of Jesus and indicated a willingness to embrace it, nothing else matters. But once at that point, we need to speak to the new believer about the importance of turning from sin, acknowledging Christ before others, beginning the new life in baptism, and receiving the promised forgiveness and the empowering presence of the Holy Spirit.

These are all the follow-through of our gospel presentation. These steps of response are not a substitute for it. Until a person is clear about what God has done for him in Christ, any talk about what he needs to do in response is premature at best and probably confusing about the real nature of the gospel.

The Next Steps in the Journey

John 3:16, our explanation of it, and our testimony about what Christ has done in our lives provide the content of the faith we want to share with those around us. Obviously, much more is involved. Likely, a lot of questions, answers, and discussion will develop out of this. In real life, we may not always have the opportunity to cover everything we want in a single setting. We need to continue to listen and demonstrate loving patience at every step without giving up on our goal of explaining more fully the hope we have in Christ.

All of the time, we want to be careful to emphasize a few critical points. Without these, our message of faith can easily be misunderstood and distorted. These include: 1) The good news is about Jesus, not us. 2) The good news is about what he did, not about what we do. 3) Following Jesus is not always easy. We face temptations. We stumble. We face tough times. He said we would. 4) But he helps us when we falter. He never abandons us. 5) Faith is a growing experience. Trusting Christ is the beginning point of a great adventure. It is not the finish line! Most importantly, we must not attempt to live the Christian life alone. We need help. Others need our help. That's what the church is all about. [Colossians 2:6-7, Romans 6:1-14, Romans 12:1-21, and Ephesians 4:17-32 all emphasize these truths.]

If friends with whom we share our faith respond positively, we will want to encourage them to take the next steps with Christ. Whatever the outcome of our initial conversation about our faith, we will want to continue to grow our friendship. If the relationship is genuine, we will continue to guide and encourage them. We will pray for them and serve them in whatever ways the Lord provides. This is how we share our faith!

***

Going Deeper—Appendix 3

1. Have you ever tried to share your faith with a friend? How did it go? How do you feel about that experience?

2. Write out your five-minute personal testimony/story of how you came to faith in Christ.

3. With your small group or class or a friend, practice walking through the gospel message using the John 3:16 plan.

Endnotes

1. Augustine of Hippo, *Confessions* (Durham, N.C.: Duke Classics, 2012; translated by E. B. Pusey), Book 1, Chapter 1, Section 1.

2. Aleksandr Solzhenitsyn, *The Gulag Archipelago*, (New York: Harper Perennial Modern Classics; Reissued Edition, 2007; translated by Thomas P. Whitney), II, 746, Kindle.

3. Anne Dillard, *Teaching a Stone to Talk* (New York: HarperCollins, 2009), 58.

4. T. S. Eliot, *Hollow Man in Poems 1909-1925*, (London: Faber and Faber, 1927), 128

5. C. S. Lewis, "They Asked for a Paper" in *Is Theology Poetry?* (London: Geoffrey Bliss, 1962), 165.

6. Lawrence O. Richards, *Creative Bible Teaching (Chicago:* Moody Press, 1976).

7. D. James Kennedy, *Evangelism Explosion*, (Carol Stream, IL: Tyndale House Publishers, 1970).

8. Augustine of Hippo, *Confessions* (Durham, N.C.: Duke Classics, 2012; translated by E. B. Pusey), Book 1, Chapter 1, Section 1.

About the Author

Will Thomas (DMin, Northern Seminary) is an adopted son of the Lone Star State. He grew up on a pig farm and worked his way through college as a construction worker. Will even spent time on the dark side as a dreaded telemarketer and a persistent Aflac agent. On the brighter side, he has served as a campus minister, pastor, church planter, college professor, and newspaper columnist. Will is the author of seven books and hundreds of magazine articles in dozens of publications, including Christianity Today, Eternity, His, Christian Standard, The Disciple, Preaching, Worldwide Challenge, Restoration Herald, and many others. In addition, his work has appeared in the widely read Chicken Soup for the Soul series. What you might not know, Will plays a six-eight power forward for the Dallas Mavericks——in his dreams.